HIGH SEASON

For Alice

HIGH
SEASON

A MEMOIR OF HEROIN
& HOSPITALITY

JIM HEARN

A R E N A
ALLEN&UNWIN

First published in Australia in 2012

Allen & Unwin
Sydney, Melbourne, Auckland, London

83 Alexander Street
Crows Nest NSW 2065
Australia
Phone: (61 2) 8425 0100
Fax: (61 2) 9906 2218
Email: info@allenandunwin.com
Web: www.allenandunwin.com

Cataloguing-in-Publication details are available from the
National Library of Australia
www.trove.nla.gov.au

ISBN 978 1 74237 841 1

Typeset in 12/14.5pt Bembo by Midland Typesetters, Australia
Printed and bound in Australia by the SOS Print + Media Group.

10 9 8 7 6 5 4

1

So I'm standing in front of my six-burner stove at Rae's on Watego's in Byron Bay and our head waiter Scotty wants to know if I'll cook a soft-shell crab for Paris Hilton that isn't deep-fried. I'm no killjoy so I say sure, it'll be wet and soggy but it'll taste like crab. Besides, it's New Year's Day and I'm feeling generous. Scotty, who knows what he's doing, takes care of her security guys with two whole fish, wok-fried vegetables, lotus-leaf rice and a couple of Peronis, then tells Paris he'll send a few things out. Scotty has a certain arrogance which goes down well with most customers.

The thing about girls and eating, particularly if they're celebrities or wannabe celebrities, is that they want the following three things when they go to a restaurant: first off, they want to have fun, which is why they travel in packs; next, they want to try a whole lot of different food, which they often share; and finally, they like all the food to look great. And what has become apparent this week with Paris Hilton, last week with Elle Macpherson and at Christmas time with Megan Gale, is that they actually have human bodies that require sustenance. The best of them know this much about themselves but many don't, and in the latter case it can mean the first rule of going out to lunch gets broken; which is to say, no one's had fun at a restaurant if they're still hungry after the meal. Doesn't matter how good the view is or the service was.

So Scotty goes all out and orders half a dozen entrees for the six girls, doubling up on two so effectively they've got eight. When it becomes obvious Paris and her little sister can really eat, Scotty, who's seen it all before, puts a rush order in for a cooked-through rib-eye steak with sweet potato mash and shitake jus, two fish of the day, three leaf salads, a main-size lemongrass-pasted Moreton Bay bug dish and, to keep the party going (as much for the other punters in the restaurant who are all busy texting their friends about who's sitting near them), we get the mains out the door as soon as the entree plates start coming back in. A share menu is a great way to eat pan-Asian cuisine anyway. It's not on a lazy Susan so you need a good waiter, but a share menu—maybe fifteen dishes for six—is a rocking good idea if everyone's there for the food rather than the Cristal. And these girls eat everything we throw at them.

The last thing they need in order to feel the day has come together for them is a great bathroom. And the bathrooms at Rae's are small but fucking great. So the girls all trip past and pile in and do whatever six girls do together in a tiny bathroom before they stumble out, giggling as they pass the kitchen where the crackhead apprentices are lined up to catch a glimpse—which is all they're going to get because the security guy, who in this instance manages things pretty well, stands in the doorway of the kitchen because he's seen what apprentice chefs are capable of. He knows that the three freaks in my kitchen, Jesse, Choc and Soda—all of whom are under twenty-one and have more body art and piercings than the Illustrated Man—are much more of a potential threat than any paparazzi. Just looking at the security guy I can see he's worried about the boys. I figure he's stood in doorways like this all over the world to deter smart-arse apprentices from yelling out, 'Paris, you want my phone number?' or 'Paris, I loved your video' or 'Paris, how were the crabs?'

But the thing about Jesse, Choc and Soda is that while they may look like punks and act like punks, they cook like angels. Not everyone can stand the heat, sweat and abuse of a busy five-star restaurant. Not all kids have the necessary survival skills to see out one busy lunch service let alone the three or four years it takes to qualify as a chef. And these kids mess up. Sometimes they're late, sometimes the police ring looking for one of them, and sometimes they crumble and cry under the pressure, but if one stuck a paring knife between another one's ribs during service, the one with the knife tickling their lungs would finish plating up their order before removing the steel from their rib cage. Okay, I exaggerate, but only slightly; these kids are tough, they can stand the heat . . .

That said, I'm starting to worry about Jesse, who looks less than pristine. He's been going hard for a couple of weeks now and although he hasn't let the line down yet, he's starting to piss everyone off with his bad attitude.

3

Jesse is the oldest of the three apprentices and the leader of the pack. It's important to the smooth running of the kitchen that Jesse doesn't get too messed up because if and when he does, he takes the other kids to hell with him. Even though I'm chef—or the old guy at the stove with a speaking part—these boys have their own sub-culture in which Jesse is the leader, and where he goes they follow. And right now, because it's high season in Byron Bay, nothing else matters other than getting through the next few weeks with whatever self-respect people can drag along behind them. The stakes are high; fuck up and walk out now, or push things too far until one of the kids break, and we're finished in this part of the world as chefs. That wouldn't matter if we'd been here six weeks or even six months, but after a couple of years we're a team and there's a certain level of expectation. Besides, Vinnie Rae would cut off our runaway legs.

Vinnie's a real treat. He's like our older brother who grew up and got rich and famous and now . . . now he's like our very rich and very demanding older brother. He looks like a blond Bob Dylan—who can surf. He came from the same kind of working-class neighbourhood as the rest of the guys in the kitchen, had the same sort of parents and same public schooling. But Vinnie was never going to stay a working-class drone. If his first job had been in the trans-port industry, he'd be a trucking magnate by now; if he'd started out in the fashion industry he'd be an international design star. But he didn't, he started in a kitchen, and now we live with the consequences of that fateful day.

The kitchen at Rae's is hot, even though the pass is open through to the bar and you can see the pandanus trees framing the blue-green sea of Watego's Beach. And it's hotter than usual lately because a heatwave has blown across town and settled into the neighbourhood like a passive-aggressive, all-seeing bully. The temperature is messing with people's heads.

Rae's is a seven-room boutique hotel with a sixty-seat restaurant and a kitchen that was never designed for commercial use. Rooms are a thousand dollars a night or more and it's not for everyone; it's expensive, but for some the value of the experience doesn't come together. That's partly because the whole time you're there you sort of feel like you're at someone's house, which is what the building was originally—a Mediterranean palace by the sea, but a house nonetheless. So the heat in the kitchen builds up. And when the breeze stops in the galley where the dishes and pots are washed, the air thickens into a vaporous steam that clings and climbs, building pressure and pushing sweat, until eventually even the toughest have to escape to take a few breaths and replace fluids.

Today it's Soda's turn to be punished; he knows he's been bad. Soda's done plenty wrong in his short life, but beneath a chemical cloud of burnt pots redemption is at hand. Soda got his weirdo name from the character in *The Outsiders*. Apparently he got called Soda at school when everyone had to read the book and it stuck. No one besides him and his family actually knows what his real name is any more. To us he's Soda and, like the fictional character, he has that wild, movie-star handsome face and easy smile that manages to keep him floating just above the grease and grime of the galley. Grandmothers, pet dogs, pussy cats—well, just about any female with

5

a pulse—are particularly partial to Soda. Once they've looked into his sea-blue eyes and seen his winning smile, they all know who's boss in the lovable stakes. Not that he tries it on with any of us chefs. In here he's just a line cook; a kitchen slave like the rest of us. But having him around, like a colourful bird in a stainless-steel cage, somehow makes it easier for us all.

Because Rae's is small, with only a handful of rooms, a great little spa and a kick-arse restaurant, the rooms are often booked out by the rich and famous. They take over the joint for a week or a weekend and enjoy the privileges of whatever success they've had, which is why lunch with Paris is not unusual and today . . . well, the relief on the security guy's face is palpable. But there's still tension in the air due to the fact they didn't tell us they were coming. And Vinnie—who owns Rae's—likes to be told such things. Scotty looks particularly stressed so I guess he hasn't been able to contact Vinnie to let him know Paris is in the house. But still, lunch service is going well. And this is despite everyone being hungover from New Year's Eve. Everyone but me. And I'm not messed up because New Year's Eve and I go way back.

2

On New Year's Eve fifteen years ago, from half past ten until four in the morning, there wasn't a single shot of smack traded on the streets of Kings Cross. There was a calm around the streets that I had never experienced before. There were a few outbursts that blew up like spot fires before being doused or moved along, but the general feeling was one of calm intensity. Everyone was either sitting at outdoor cafes or leaning against doorjambs or slouched into the crevices of buildings, watching . . . waiting . . . for the dope to turn up. Everyone agreed it would; everyone knew someone who knew something who said it was travelling; and all anyone could do was wait. Some people couldn't sit it out and they blew across town or traded down to alcohol or something else low-grade, but for the purists, for the ones who needed heroin and nothing less, it was just one more challenge in a life of crime. The actual countdown at midnight to the birth of the new year was strictly for the punters. And there were plenty of them, laughing, kissing, drinking, pinching,

7

poking and blowing off steam. Truly, if there's a bigger amateur's night than New Year's Eve, I haven't heard about it.

It was about four am when the dope hit. There were still a lot of partygoers out and about, and for about twenty minutes they ruled the streets as every hooker, hustler and drugstore cowboy moved through the crowd and disappeared into boltholes and mirror-balled rooms, beneath stairwells and stoops, up to rooftops and into hour-stay motel rooms. And because everyone was so utterly fucking grateful the dope had turned up, there wasn't a lot of pushing and shoving; there was respect among the crew that we'd waited this one out; we'd come through something, together. And the word was, the dope was good. It was grade-one, straight-off-the-boat, pink-fucking-rocks. It could have been one hundred percent battery acid and no one would have minded. Every single hopeless junkie in the neighbourhood would have shot it up and hoped to get one last ping before the lights went out.

The weirdest thing was, I discovered while sitting in a hotel room in Hampton Court where a hooker lived with her three-year-old son and a bunch of other low-life scum, the dope really *was* good. As soon as I put my shot away—a larger than usual shot given the utter torment of having waited so long—the rush to my head was better than any I had ever experienced before. And while I'd dropped plenty of times and lived to tell the tale, this was different. Everything went quiet as I pushed the fit home, pulled it out, then instinctively stood up and started for the door. In that moment of bliss, I knew this was as close as I was ever going to get to the sensation of my first shot, no matter how long I kept looking or how much dope I continued to use. It was such a pure, utterly pinging stone that I felt every organ in my body slowing, starting to close down, like . . . they wanted to stop functioning. Another thing I knew was that unless I managed to get across the road and into the club where Caroline, my girlfriend at the time, had been waiting for several hours—without so much as a phone call—she was going to be so powerfully pissed off I might never get close to those unbelievably perfect tits again. And the third thing I knew was that, if I was going to drop from an overdose, it was of the utmost importance that I didn't do so in that room.

Of course it was rude to just up and leave but I didn't give a fuck. The pressing nature of my insights motivated me away from any concerns for etiquette and towards the safety of either dying alone in a darkened laneway or collapsing into Caroline's milky chest.

It wasn't until I hit the ground at the entrance of the hotel that I realised I wouldn't make it to the club. And the bitumen, as I hurtled towards it, became a landscape in miniature; layers of rock-hard chewing gum and tiny pot-holes morphed into a patched history that blew up into a storyboard of loves gone wrong and addictive despair. And then nothing.

Until I awoke at St Vincent's Hospital with a team of medical staff screaming over the top of me, 'Breathe!'

To which I replied, 'Fuck off—I can breathe, you idiots.'

Stuff gratitude. They knew the score about giving a junkie Narcan, a drug that immediately nullifies the effects of opiates.

To go from being utterly stoned to awaken more straight than you've been for many years . . . well, it's a shock to the system and one that medical staff in emergency wards are ready for. Never mind that the good hard-working doctors had just saved my life—I was stoned, you morons!

The moment after I began breathing again, all the medical staff except one took off in order to deal with the next crisis while I got a lecture and a bright yellow envelope, the contents of which I was advised to read if I didn't want to end up dead. The doctor who'd stayed behind asked if I'd seen anything on the other side. But I hadn't. It was just blackness and nothing.

3

There's a gentle two-foot swell down at Watego's Beach where old-timers on longboards slide to the right, two steps forward, one step back, then disappear out of view of the restaurant pass. There are no walls to the restaurant at Rae's. Diners sit around a semicircular space, and what separates them from the other punters, who are out enjoying the best of what Byron Bay has to offer, is more cultural than physical. If it rains the plastic sheets are flung down off the roof but otherwise it's all fresh sea air and envious looks from those doing the lighthouse walk.

Crisp linen drapes the tables and pink frangipanis, which have fallen from the ancient tree at the entrance to the restaurant, litter the timber floor. Lunch is fully underway with Paris and Nicky and their entourage. Scotty is calm about service but scratching at his bald head because he still can't raise Vinnie on the phone.

'How are the girls?' I ask him.

'Yeah, yeah, good,' he replies. 'Still fucking hungry though. Who said models don't eat?'

'They're not models, mate. They're—'

'Yeah, whatever. They want a couple more green papaya salads and another soft-shell crab.'

'Tell me she wants it fried this time,' I say.

'She wants it however it's on the menu, Chef,' Scotty says, grinning faintly.

'Correct answer,' I say, winking at Choc, whose job it is to get the crab underway.

'You're a genius, Chef. They love it all,' Scotty carries on.

'Correct again, Scotty. And I don't care what people say about you, mate—I think you're a top bloke,' I tell him, taking the piss. 'Vinnie called back yet?'

'Fuck off,' Scotty replies, and heads back to the floor.

Jesse, Choc and Soda are surprisingly impressed with Paris, Nicky and their friends. Their earlier cynicism has all but disappeared, even Jesse's, which is actually a little disturbing. No one is used to Jesse being anything other than a relentless piss-taker and for him to be a fan, or at least not outrageously nasty about the girls, is high praise where we come from. And we do all agree that there's something about the girls. They're not so much sexy as surprisingly classy. Given that our perceptions of Paris Hilton have been gleaned from tabloids and gossip mags, the boys in the kitchen are a little surprised to find that Paris and the girls look rich, rather than crass. And really, given the wealth and privilege that she must have grown up with, it shouldn't come as such a shock. Even though they are casually dressed, they exude a different aura to your average pretty girl. They look and smell and move like princess cats, like American royalty might.

Jesse's seeming affection for Paris has me suspicious, though. Since I've shuffled him over to the larder section for lunch service rather than have him do woks, his usual station, I would have expected him to be rambling on in his semi-angry whine that has the rest of the world somehow indebted to him. And it's not that I don't relate to that, it's just that I'm a little too old to get away with such banter now if it isn't done in a self-deprecating way. But Jesse's not whining, and that's odd. Something's going on and I don't like not knowing what it is. Call it being a control freak or a pain in the arse or just plain nosey, but I've found that if I'm not up to speed on what's happening with the crew, they often surprise me by leaving suddenly or taking a week off or performing some other random act that throws the line, and therefore the kitchen, into disarray.

'How long on that *som dtam*, Jesse?' I call.

'Two minutes, Chef,' he yells back.

'Choc, how long on the crab?'

'One minute, Chef.'

'Jesse, get the salad up in one,' I demand.

'Yes, Chef!'

'You like larder, don't you, Jesse?' I say, trying to tease a reaction out of him, something that might give me a clue as to what's going on.

'No, Chef, but I enjoyed sleeping in so I don't give a fuck if I have to do larder.'

'Jesse doesn't give a fuck, people. Did everyone hear that?' I call to the crew.

'Yes, Chef,' they respond.

'You've been sleeping in a lot lately, Jesse. Have you got a new boyfriend?'

13

'Yes, Chef,' he says, not biting.

'Well, we'd all like to meet him someday so we can see why your section has gone to shit.'

'I'd bring him in, Chef, but I'm afraid you might steal him off me,' Jesse answers.

'Give me that salad,' I order.

'Yes, Chef,' says Jesse, turning around from his section to put the salad on the pass in front of me. And as he turns, I see that he doesn't actually look that well. He looks upset or hurt. And that's not normally Jesse's go. Like I said, these kids are tough, they can handle the heat, but intuitively I pull back on the piss-taking and get back to business.

'Choc, clap that order out and let's go up on table four,' I call.

'Yes, Chef.' And Choc claps twice for the floor staff to come collect the food. (I don't know why we clap at Rae's rather than ring a bell like every other kitchen I've ever worked in, but like a lot of traditions there doesn't have to be a reason—it's just how it's done.)

Scotty comes in and collects the soft-shell crab and green papaya salads for Paris's table.

'Oh, Scotty? Vinnie called for you, mate, but we told him you were busy,' I say.

'Fuck off, Chef,' Scotty growls.

'He'll understand, mate. I'm sure he will,' I lie.

'It's not my fucking problem his phone's off,' Scotty says, shaking his head. It's a headshake that's resigned to knowing Vinnie won't see it that way. Basically everything is Scotty's fault, and while that might not be rational it's how it is at Rae's.

The boys in the kitchen are all looking at Scotty and smiling slightly nervously at the thought of Vinnie turning up unexpectedly and ripping into him.

It may seem a little juvenile or even cruel the way chefs and waiters take the piss out of each other, but it's just a way to distract themselves from the physical punishment of working in a commercial kitchen. The life of a chef is very demanding on the body. As a person gets older, male or female, the reality of performing for sixteen hours a day, six or seven days a week, begins to lose a little of its gloss. It's like, here I am at Rae's on New Year's Day after doing about ten days straight—each day a double lunch and dinner service—and my legs no longer want to play. My Achilles tendon is refusing—just straight-out refusing—to bend. And it's not just my body; my mind is constantly buzzing with so many details that require thinking about in order to maintain a semi-organised kitchen that absolutely none of it makes any sense. My nervous system is shot after so many years in the kitchen, and the idea of not walking with a weird gait or of having a stomach that's not contending with sixty-nine different kinds of food is a novel thought which, in my quieter moments, forms a very pleasant fantasy.

Scotty tries phoning Vinnie again. He knows Vinnie will want to look after Paris, maybe even buy her a drink. It's not as if Scotty hasn't got enough to worry about in terms of Vinnie's relationships with difficult celebrities. Bret Easton Ellis, who's telling anyone who'll listen how cute those Australian shrink-wrapped copies of *American Psycho* are, is staying in penthouse one. For some obscure reason he has chosen the Byron Bay Writers Festival to launch his latest book. Apparently it's the first writers' festival he has attended anywhere in the world and he seems determined to make the most of the experience. On top of that, Baz Luhrmann is in penthouse two with CM and the kids, and there's a whole scene going on between Bret and Baz because Bret, during some interview, told the audience that *The Great Gatsby* was never going to make a decent film; how books and films are fundamentally different things. And he knew that Baz had the rights to *The Great Gatsby*. This has made for a tense atmosphere during breakfast, when the restaurant is reserved for hotel guests. It's been Scotty's job to ensure they never cross paths. And the thing about Paris is that, while everyone loves Paris, she's not staying in the hotel and no one bothered to tell us she was coming in for lunch.

To add to Scotty's stress, David Bromley is painting a wall in room seven. It's a nude scene. Vinnie has installed Bromley's canvases in the foyer and up the central circular staircase. Vinnie and David are old mates and when the idea of the mural came up there was a lot of good cheer about the concept of naked models functioning as muses, expensive champagne and general good vibes. It's just that now there are six highly attractive, very tall and completely naked girls wandering about the place. Bromley is pissed off because they won't sit still and while Scotty is not someone who would normally dismiss the demands of a naked woman, he's not exactly relishing the added pressure of fetching tuna carpaccio with fresh wasabi for the tipsy girls. And ice cubes! What is it with models and champagne with ice?

If Vinnie were here, it would all be sorted because he understands that hospitality begins with a host's capacity to be hospitable. Hospitality is defined as the relationship between a host and a guest, and Vinnie is the person I've learnt the most from about hospitality. His genius has always been to get the best out of people while simultaneously letting them know their efforts, while good, are just below his high expectations. He is both outrageously successful and ruthlessly charming. His riches are built upon inspiring in others a previously untapped ability to do unpaid overtime, as well as his capacity to attract a stellar—and loaded—clientele.

After a couple of successful restaurants and a raging nightclub in Brisbane, Vinnie bought the building that is now Rae's on Watego's in Byron Bay and took it from a million-dollar home-stay to a twenty-five-million-dollar palace. He owns other businesses, houses and restaurants, and still insists on driving a Porsche. He is a perfectionist and doesn't suffer either fools or the too-intelligent gladly.

Despite Condé Naste having rated Rae's on Watego's one of the twenty-five best boutique hotels in the world, Vinnie generally has a poor relationship with the Australian media and their various ratings systems. The *Sydney Morning Herald* and the more local rags mostly fail to find cause to celebrate Rae's particular style. Not that Vinnie cares. He is a man consumed more by the mechanics of trade and the virtues of pleasure than the dull art of public relations. Which is something of a paradox, and also an uncommon trait.

Many chefs and proprietors at the fine-dining end of hospitality are so obsessed with the status that a good review can bring that everything else, including food costs and good business sense, disappears at a hint of criticism. There appears to be an assumption that what makes a restaurant successful has more to do with how the media represents it than with notions of what constitutes hospitality. The lack of self-respect displayed by many head chefs and proprietors at various award nights only confirms the idea that the media is somehow judge and jury of all things hospitality.

Working at Rae's on Watego's isn't for everyone. People get to see the full extent of their limitations pretty quickly. And if you do want to work at Rae's, you catch on pretty quick it's all about Vinnie. It doesn't matter if you're head chef, maître d' or hotel manager, any praise is only ever slightly deflected your way and any problems are reason enough for rip-down humiliation. Vinnie is expert in the art of humiliation. He palpably enjoys tearing into those he perceives as having an ego problem. When things are going well, as they often are, it is only ever because he has afforded you the space to reach such heights. Never forget that you were nothing prior to arriving at Rae's.

Vinnie insists on a certain level of adaptability in his staff. Evidence of such adaptability is expected to be displayed via daily rituals in which Vinnie injects some unexpected demand into proceedings in a bid to test a person's capacity to absorb chaos. He does this because he figures if he can do it, you should be able to as well. It's an expectation thing. The idea that he's paying a chef simply to turn up and cook is anathema to his sense of value. And should a chef not be the type of person to wilfully value-add at every opportunity, Vinnie has a million great ideas that will either inspire a capacity for more mercantile thinking, or reveal a chef's particular weakness to everyone at the hotel.

Vinnie's expectations are that each and every plate be crystal clean and correctly warmed; each and every sauce be perfectly executed and served in a timely fashion; and that each and every hidden corner of the kitchen be free of grease and grime. The time of day or number of staff in the kitchen has no bearing on whether these expectations are achievable. Such standards are immutable, constantly reinforced and become—in the staff with sufficient resilience—the dominant voice inside their heads.

Of course, Vinnie realises that people have partners and children and a life outside of work, but he has no real interest in such things except in how they might affect his hotel. Spot fires from those distressed others will, on occasion, burst into flame and threaten the order of things. And during such fiery moments, benevolent Vinnie will magically appear and throw a dog a bone—or at least the appearance of a bone—but only for staff members who have survived a certain length of time.

Perhaps the reason Vinnie demands such perfection from his staff is that, unlike us, he knows what hedonism feels like. To successfully deliver a pleasurable stay to a sophisticated clientele requires sound knowledge of what your competitors are offering. Rae's is not the most expensive boutique hotel in the country, but it does offer a premium service at a premium location. And the thing is, none of his staff will ever know what it feels like to stay at a place like Rae's, which is why Vinnie sees it as his responsibility to regale us with stories about all the fabulous hotels he regularly stays in and why—the implication being that we greasers don't have what it takes to go to the next level. If only we could experience what staying in a real five-star hotel was all about!

You will experience hedonism at Rae's on Watego's, as long as you don't get stressed about abusing the platinum Amex. Given that a decent room will cost about fifteen hundred dollars a night, a reasonable bottle of champagne a thousand and dinner a couple of hundred more, it's when you wake up and get screwed another fifty for breakfast that you're going to be tested. Nothing comes free at Rae's. The pain just keeps coming and it's the guests who can continue to say yes to every little thing who are going to get close to attaining a state of hedonistic transcendence. Vinnie sees it as his job to ensure your stay is equal parts pleasure and pain. Come check-out time, you're going to feel a little bit slapped around no matter how rich you are, and if you're ready for anything after a weekend at Rae's, it's a refreshed sense of the value of modesty and the virtue of prudence rather than a feeling you've left an itch unscratched.

4

I was fifteen when I entered my first restaurant kitchen. My parents had divorced a while before, and my mother had replaced the red dirt of Mount Isa for the red lights of a different town. Somewhere along the line she'd organised this, my first full-time job. I had no comprehension of what was required of an apprentice chef and little understanding of the future implications of being there.

Oliver's Restaurant wasn't exactly on the gastronomic map; it had received no stars, hats or write-ups of any distinction. And quite possibly, like many restaurants of its kind, it has long since closed and reopened half a dozen times under different names, headed by chefs dreaming vastly different culinary dreams. And dreams are what hospitality is all about. While many people like to think of hospitality as a service industry responsible for addressing the functionary needs of the body, for those on the inside it can be a weird and wonderful dreamscape of ungodly hours, ridiculous pressures, unkind owners, absurd customers, torture, humiliation and occasional moments of brilliance. The thrill of getting all the sections of a busy kitchen firing, and putting it all together on the night, is like no other thrill I know.

Glenn, my first head chef, was fresh out of cooking school and had an unashamed passion for red cordial laced with methylated spirits. On the rocks. He had a ginger handlebar moustache and a temperament I would come to understand as a particular type. A busy, nervy confusion of energy, Glenn was somehow, despite his jittery nature, easy to get on with. He figured if life had sent you to the inside of his kitchen, you were pretty much fucked and there was no reason to make things worse. Glenn also possessed a capacity for kindness, though it insisted on coming undone during every lunch and dinner service. And hell really is a stressed-out, angry head chef in a no-good restaurant during a busy service. Forget about fine-dining celebrity head chefs—we'll get to those freaks later—back there, in that out-of-the-way Townsville diner, hell had another name.

So it happened that, as I stood in front of my first open coolroom, I found I couldn't move. My senses were being assaulted by an unreasonable number of smells and my body refused to function until I could reorganise the odours into one thing, one smell. And that particular coolroom odour was to repeat itself over the next twenty-five years in inexplicable ways. It was as if this coolroom was all possible coolrooms; its stored ingredients, its sauces, produce, pastes, meats, condiments, cheeses, seafood and mould melded into one archetypal olfactory sensation. I've since cooked in Western, Eastern,

Middle Eastern and Asian restaurants and, while the food has obviously tasted and smelt differently, the coolrooms all smelt like the one at Oliver's Restaurant.

'Shut the coolroom, faggot,' said Glenn in his semi-kind, before-service voice.

So I slid the coolroom door shut and Glenn, who had his gee-whizzo-kiddo stare on, asked, 'Where's the butter, fag?' (I know it's an offensive, puerile and ridiculous turn of phrase, but in Glenn's world, everyone and everything was a faggot—except Glenn. If you were Glenn, you were surrounded by, as it were, homosexual objects.)

'Sorry, Chef, I forgot.'

'Jesus fucking Christ, fag . . .' Glenn barged past me into the coolroom, ripped the butter from the shelf and slammed the door so hard the coolroom bell rang. There's a bell on the outside of every coolroom door which is installed to attract the attention of people in the kitchen should someone get locked inside. Which happens a lot more than it should.

'But-ter,' Glenn droned in the manner of someone with a mental impairment, as if I didn't know what butter was.

So there I was, in my first restaurant kitchen, suffering my first kitchen humiliation. I was a mere kid, who had just left my eighth less-than-average school having failed half my subjects. I had absolutely no fucking idea what I was doing, or how to behave, or what constituted the difference between an outright moron and apprentice of the year. But the thing about being confused in a restaurant kitchen, with its stainless steel and fluorescent lights and its out-the-back status, was that I was not alone. Many people like me found employment, and a life, inside their version of Oliver's.

'You're a moron,' said Chef Glenn, testing me.

'Yes, Chef,' I mumbled.

'What?'

'Yes, Chef,' I yelled, more vigorously this time.

Chef Glenn nodded, semi-impressed.

And I couldn't help but smile as the ageing, seen-it-all-before waiter ripped the first of many lunch checks from his order book.

Besides the smell of a coolroom, the second archetypal smell of a restaurant kitchen is that of a burnt bamboo skewer. Chefs all over the world light the burner they want to use with a bamboo skewer lit using a pilot light or other gas burner. Then they shake out the flame on the skewer or blow it out or snub it in the wok station water and the smell . . . I don't know what it is, I just know it's the same everywhere and it's the signal that the day's work has started. Everyone knows that the six boxes of matches and two lighters that were neatly placed in the service-is-starting-get-ready positions are out the back in the storeroom with the empty beer bottles, wine glasses and ashtrays that accumulated after the end of service the night before. They'll be shoved under dirty aprons or empty cardboard boxes.

It's not that every service ends in a celebration, it's just that at the end of every service two things happen: chefs get changed out of their kitchen whites and into their street clothes, and the service that has just finished unravels in their minds and in their conversation. If it's been a massive service, you'll be having a drink and chatting, laughing, taking the piss and generally talking it up, and the bonhomie has been known to extend beyond the mechanics of getting changed. There's a tipping point, which is often just a matter of agreeing to a second drink, that signals to everyone to get the fuck out now if you have to . . . and if you don't, you'll be going to bed with the words, 'Where the fuck are the matches, faggot?' ringing in your swimming brain.

My first pay cheque stretched far enough to buy a carton of beer and some fancy Italian deli food. I got outrageously drunk on a beach in Townsville and danced and vomited and drank some more. When I look back now it seemed a time of confusion and hopelessness; a time when alcohol seemed to bring me undone in a childish fashion each time I drank. I vaguely remember older, wiser waiters and maître d's, chefs and bearded kitchen hands, patting me on the back, ruffling my hair, telling me that it'd all work out; that I'd be fine.

Yet what I came to see over the coming months and years was that despite working like an adult, taking on responsibilities and more hours than was reasonable for someone my age, I was a kid who hadn't or couldn't yet come to terms with what had gone before. I was both a child and a teenager and the stories of my family contin-ued to inform who I was and how I felt, and might even be the reason I drank so much at such a young age.

It is impossible to write about my early years in hospi-tality without including a description, a sense, of the life

I had come from. Hospitality for me is and has always been a transitional space. Kitchens come and go, people slide in and out of a chef's life, '. . . until the next gig'. My inherent capacity to leave a job fairly easily, to come undone and move on, was a continuation of a pattern established from childhood.

When my parents divorced it was my mother who left my father. Who leaves whom is perhaps the most telling signifier at the end of a relationship. Of course many couples like to say that it was mutual, that each of the parties came out of it with their pride and self-respect intact, but anyone old enough to have fallen in love knows that's bullshit. Someone gets done over and someone does the doing over. In my family's case, my mother, after having six children and not missing a Sunday mass for sixteen years, cut loose with a vengeance and somehow found herself working in brothels around Kings Cross. This isn't really as dramatic as it sounds. The thing about being a prostitute is that for most people it's such a fantastical notion it's hard to get your head around what it entails. The reality of such a life, as least the backstage view of such a life, is that it's like most other jobs. There's the usual dramas, boring bits, good days and bad; it's just that there's not a whole lot of people you can talk to about what happened at the office.

I always felt that the reason my mother left was because my father sacrificed his family in order to make the world a better place. I don't think he ever set out to lose the ones he loved, but like many others of his generation he got caught up in the ideological fever of the times, which in his case translated into a strange mix of idealism, social justice and Catholicism. What set my father apart from others in our community, who also found great meaning in those topics, was his decision to act rather than simply talk. When I arrived home from school one day as a six-year-old kid to discover our house on a four-acre block had been sold, my childhood was essentially over. The proceeds of the sale were to be given to a family less fortunate than ours and we were urged to believe that our needs would be met without the requirement of material wealth.

Thus began an epic family journey through five rented houses, eight schools and three regional Queensland towns until finally my mother decided she'd had enough and left. And when she left, she didn't look back.

There is no history of chefs or professional cooks in my family. No tradition to explain why Mum had sent me to work at Oliver's Restaurant.

5

Despite my rusted Achilles tendons, sore back, aching feet and general lethargy, during the lunch service at Rae's these things become a distant memory. I'm calling the pass, tossing pans, opening and closing the oven, squatting to open the reach-in service fridge in order to pull out another portion of fish or beef or a container of herbs. It's as if in this corner of the universe, I don't have to think. There's nothing to worry about other than the immediacy of the next order and the ten after that and the temperature of various pots, sauces, woks, oil and protein. My *mise en place* is so fucking set—by which I mean so full and unlikely to run out—that I don't care how many punters turn up for lunch. When you know you're set and you can trust the rest of the line to be equally prepared there's nothing better than being busy. Every guest is getting the real deal today; there are no short cuts or half measures. Fuck that—this is the first day of a brand-new year and it's all about fresh starts and clean slates and everyone staying or dining at Rae's is getting nothing but the best.

As the service rolls on, though, it's apparent that Jesse is falling further and further behind on larder. Jesse is not a salad and leaf guy; he's a smoking wok and protein man. Jesse can get the job done in any section, including mine, but he's also a kid and his life is a fucking mess and whatever is going on with him is affecting his capacity to stay organised.

'Soda!' I yell in the direction of the galley. 'Give Jesse a hand for ten minutes.'

'Yes, Chef,' Soda yells back, happy to be released from the hell of a million dirty pots and plates.

'You got that cutlery through, Sodapop?' Scotty shouts into the steam.

'Yeah.' Soda tips the tray of silver noisily into a bucket that he passes to Scotty before joining Jesse on larder.

And Jesse doesn't make a big deal about it. If you're in the shit, you're in the shit. The only thing you want to do when you're there is get out of it and he starts Soda off prepping the *mise en place* that his section has run out of.

'Choc,' I call, 'let's go on tables six and seven.'

'Yes, Chef!' He pulls a whole fish out of its soy bath and drops it into the deep-fryer.

Choc deserves to spend some time in the bright lights of the wok section anyway. While he's below Jesse in the kitchen hierarchy, he's a good chef and it's pleasing to see him going so well during such a busy service.

'Scotty,' I yell as the head waiter leaves the kitchen with his bucket of clean but unpolished cutlery.

'Not now, Chef,' he says over his shoulder.

'I've got a phone card if you need it, mate.'

Scotty is stalling Paris and the girls on ordering dessert, which is something they are apparently desperate for. And he is doing this for two very good reasons: he doesn't want them to leave before he manages to get in touch with Vinnie; and he knows that Jesse and Soda, who have to slide down the line to the pastry section after they finish on larder, are anything but ready.

As lunch progresses I'm getting a little scared by just how much these girls are eating—and they're enjoying the food. Those plates are coming back empty. It's not some anorexic trip where people order a whole lot of food and get stoned by pushing things around the crockery and refusing to eat any of it. Maybe it's just a hangover thing? Although they don't look hungover—they look fresh and bright and innocent. And even though I'm sure they're not all those things, I can't help thinking there's some serious disconnect between the media representations of Paris Hilton and the girls sitting in the restaurant.

The word seems to have spread among the locals and those who are keen to have lunch with Paris are floating into the joint wrapped in their Donna Karan kaftans and four-hundred-dollar sandals. The worst of it is that most of them are friends of Vinnie's and pretty soon it's going to be a full house . . . minus the guy with his name over the door.

Scotty is back with the girls' dessert order, and he doesn't look well.

'You need an aspirin, mate?' I ask as the phone starts ringing.

'Give me two coconut cakes, one sorbet, one chocolate and one tasting plate,' Scotty replies.

'That'll be Vinnie now,' I say, nodding at the phone.

'Fuck him if it is. There's nothing I can do about it.'

And he's right. We all know that. But that's not the point. This is Rae's and everything is Scotty's fault. And it's not that Vinnie is some random star-fucker or people pleaser—he's got more famous friends than he knows what to do with. It's just that he takes his role of being a host and hotelier seriously and he knows that a few good words from Paris Hilton is worth more than a toque awarded by a Sydney broadsheet.

Scotty is only on the phone for a few seconds before he's back in the kitchen.

'The police are the phone for you, Jesse.'

'Oh, fuck off,' replies Jesse.

'Tell them he's busy,' I joke.

'You tell them,' Scotty says as he disappears.

'Choc, take over from Jesse.'

'I've got to finish this order, Chef,' Jesse argues.

'Go talk to them, Jesse,' I tell him. 'Choc, finish that order off with Soda and then both of you get the girls' desserts out.'

'Yes, Chef!'

'Fuck!' yells Jesse as he angrily kicks dirty pots out of his way as he leaves the kitchen to answer the phone.

'Table ten's entrees are up, Chef,' Soda says as he places two perfectly prepared spanner crab salads with red *nahm jim* on the pass.

'Nice. They look great. Now get those fucking desserts out,' I order.

Jesse storms back into the kitchen. 'I've got to move the car or they're going to tow me,' he says.

'Fuck, Jesse,' I say. 'Where did you park?'

'Across the driveway next door. No one ever uses it.' He sounds pissed off, like it's perfectly resonable to block the driveway of someone who's paying ten thousand dollars a week to rent the house next door to Rae's.

'It's fucking lunch service on New Year's Day and you've got to go move your fucking car. Not cool, Jesse.' I'm stating the obvious.

'I'll be back in a minute, Chef.' Jesse grabs the keys off Soda. And trust me when I say Soda should not have the keys. He's in a whole other world of pain with the police for matters regarding cars, and for him to be even holding keys is criminal.

'Tell me you didn't drive the car to work, Soda,' I say, all serious.

'It's fine, Chef. I'm on it,' Jesse assures me as he bolts out of the kitchen to go move his heap-of-shit car.

'Nah,' Soda drawls completely unconvincingly before cracking a smile that would split cream.

'Fuck!' I yell.

'Nah, really, Chef. It's all right. It looks like I'm going to get off that last rap if I help out down at the youth centre,' Soda says.

'Oh, right,' I say, like *it's me you're talking to, idiot*. 'Help the kiddies out down at the centre, eh? You trashed a BMW, mate, and wrote off a small business. I'm not sure teaching the Under 12 football team to cook pasta is going to cut it.'

'Apparently it will, Chef,' Soda says, his blue eyes flashing mischief, as if he can't believe it either.

'Yeah, crazy fucking world, ain't it, Sodapop? Finish that check off, for chrissake. How long, how long, how long?'

That's the last call I give before I start getting all fucked up and serious. And really, no one likes me when I get that way, so the boys pull out all stops and start calling back like they're actually serious line cooks rather than fuckwit petty gangsters.

'Thirty seconds, Chef!' Choc calls as he places the first of the girls' dessert orders up to the pass.

'Fucking Jesse,' I grumble to no one in particular. 'That's the last piece of bullshit news I need in relation to that guy. What the fuck is his problem?' I yell into the blazing heat of my stove, where all six burners are roasting the air. Exhaust fans are roaring above my sweating head and two million dirty frypans and stainless-steel bowls are jostling for an inch of bench space. Suddenly it's all very hot and crowded in my little corner of the world. Not even Vinnie could find a way to describe lunch service as anything but a success though. And it may just be that I feel pissed off because I don't even have half a minute to spend covered in glory before Jesse pulls focus back on to himself over some new bullshit newsflash.

'Go easy, Chef,' Scotty barks into my personal space. 'There's only one parking spot outside Deke's house.'

And Scotty—who after years of training from Vinnie is now an expert at ending a man's adrenaline rush or smashing the first hint of anything that looks or smells remotely like ego—is referring to the fact that because

I got to work before all the other fuckwit cooks in my kitchen, I got to park in the one secret spot at Watego's.

'Well, fuck me, Scotty!' I snarl after him as he disappears out to the restaurant. 'Who said crime doesn't pay? Service!' I clap twice as the boys pile the desserts onto the pass.

6

The Bondi Hotel is a landmark building on the beach-front at Bondi in Sydney. For some reason, it seemed more of an institution twenty years ago than it does today, somehow less try-hard and more gracious. Over the years it's had some unsympathetic renovations and has been crowded into the background by some ridiculous architecture either side of it. When I started work there it was like walking into a dreamscape; like thirty-five-millimetre film rather than HD video. The place didn't just smell of beer and cigarettes, the odours were ghosts that held the joint together. It had endless nooks and crannies, rickety staircases that led nowhere, bathrooms which weren't used any more (or at least not for their intended purpose) and a drug-dealing scene that was the envy of all the other pubs of Sydney's eastern suburbs.

In the late eighties, the hotel was a haven for Kiwis fresh off the boat from New Zealand, Pacific Islanders (who you learnt quickly were very different to Maoris) and leather-clad bikers. Though its twenty-four-hour trading licence wasn't used regularly, come public holidays and long weekends the hotel never closed. Christmas in particular was a fucking blast.

Staff turnover was high. The ultra-violence of knife fights at three am, glasses smashed into faces and syringe-clogged urinals wasn't for everyone. But this was how I pictured heaven.

The Bondi Hotel, which I'll forever associate with the beginning of what I like to call my 'heroin period', was without doubt one of the greatest times of my life. The people there weren't just loose, they were off their fucking chops. It was a fantasyland of good times and crazy nights and pool-table politics. This was before pokies ruined everything great about public bars. Back then there were no beeping robots with round-eyed suckers attached. People talked, drank beer and took the piss. They also fought, argued, ate and fell asleep.

But what really mattered at the Bondi back then was playing pool, and I got good at it. I would often be so stoned for such long periods of time that the pressed metal ceilings would become animated, guiding my shots from twenty feet above, the sheer scale of the place adding to the surreal feel of dark and boozy nights. And when a person who wasn't familiar with the etiquette walked into the pub, they would be a little wide-eyed, clearly wondering, *Are you guys for real?* And the thing is, we were.

The three main bars of the hotel were run by different, sometimes warring but generally peaceful factions. The Kiwis had the public bar, the Pacific Islanders had the poolroom and back bar, and the bikers had the front bar. What I mean by 'had' is that they controlled the sale of drugs in that part of the hotel. These guys had Uzi machine guns, sawn-off shotguns and the capacity to inflict such brutal physical pain with their fists and clubs that the idea of someone or some group imposing some other form of order over the top of what existed would have seemed absurd in the time I was there. The police would raid the joint from time to time but otherwise we had the place to ourselves. And because many of the regulars had so much money from selling so many drugs, the proprietors, along with everyone else, were pretty happy.

The kitchen was busy, though the food was basic. This was not a Weight Watchers club; there were some very fucking large people around the hotel who had a penchant for large slabs of beef with buckets of vegetables and sauce. Food costs were out the window. The focus was on keeping the blood sugar levels of very imposing men at a level whereby they considered me friendly. What the fuck did I know? I was a kid from Central Queensland who, while capable of taking a swing, was much happier beneath the umbrella of existing arrangements. They let me know what they liked and how they liked it and I did my best to provide. It was a simple arrangement really, and I'm pleased to say I got to call some of these people my friends. And my dealers.

Anyone who tells you that the experience of being high on heroin is no good either hasn't tried it or is just getting clean and wishes they didn't have to. Heroin, particularly in the early stages of your first addiction, is one of life's great pleasures. If you survive. Many don't. We've all lost friends from the needle and spoon, and I'm not intending to endorse the drug but simply describe how it was for me. And if the story starts well, the ending's a whole other thing.

JD was one of the smaller Pacific Islanders, and it was JD who suggested I might like to try some smack. I said why not and handed over the thirty bucks, and he was back in a few minutes with some packeted syringes and a foil of smack. I watched as he poured the powder into a spoon—which we had plenty of in the kitchen—squirted in some water, mixed it up with the butt of a syringe then sucked it up through a cigarette butt filter into the plastic barrel. He carefully pointed out the exact quantity, squirted half back into the spoon, and pushed the needle into a vein on his forearm. He was very business-like, JD, pulling the fit out of his arm then throwing it into the kitchen bin before repeating the exercise for me with a fresh pick. Frankly I was stunned he could perform such tasks given what was happening to the pupils of his eyes. But JD didn't seem to notice, sort of coughing a couple times while he indicated I should squeeze my bicep and pump my hand in order to get a vein. The sight of such pristine blood pipes got him more animated than anything else that happened that day, and quick as the Red Cross, JD pushed the fit into the fattest vein on my arm, drew back some blood, and plunged the white lady home.

The sensation of my heart pumping heroin through my bloodstream was profound. Prior to that moment, life as I understood it could be depicted as a series of random sketches that formed a clumsy whole. Now it had all come together in the most warmly felt of ways, like hollandaise sauce. The sunlight was not simply light, but a matter of hues, shades and heat. My limbs, with their niggling pains and clumsiness, became coordinated. My mind was aware but not critical; accepting, peaceful . . . relaxed. And after the pinging rush, there was no confusion or anxiety; no physical pain or nagging voice in my head drawing my attention to ridiculous details. And it was perhaps this quieting of my racing mind that brought me the most relief. It hit me that it was okay to let go occasionally, all right to kick back and let things slide. Until that shot of smack, life had been a survival course, full of unexpected plot points, hair-raising bends and curves, unforeseen sniper attacks. It was wearying. I was ready for a little *I don't give a fuck* time. And as I lolled back onto a milk crate and stared in wonder at the magic of a slowly revolving ceiling fan, I reasoned that if being loved could ever feel half as good as this, then I had never been loved.

On one level, the next eight or nine years were pretty repetitive. And while it's true that nothing's as sweet as the first time, not all of it was bad either. There are plenty of junkies who have used more dope than I've spilt; it's just that everyone's different about these things. What I had no problems with was the culture of being an addict. I seemed to slide on in there like I was born to the role. And maybe I was.

During my time at the Bondi, other than learning how to use heroin and various other cocktails of drink and drugs,

I also learnt how to cook a steak. And let's be clear about this: steak here is beef. It's not pork or lamb or chicken or duck or fish. Steak comes from cows and the best beef for eating is Angus. And I'm not into discussing this with any real openness to other ways of knowing beef; far too many chefs and backyard barbeque cooks think they know a lot about beef and, to put it bluntly, they don't. Cooking beef is one of the most underrated skills a chef might acquire. How hard can it be? Let me tell you, cooking steaks, particularly the thick eye fillet or tenderloin, how the customer orders it is quite an art. And the reason for this is that every steak is different. There is no such thing as a perfectly timed steak and I know plenty of restaurants that buy portion-controlled tender cuts to try to get around the difficulty of inconsistent portions of meat, but they aren't worth the premium.

Cooking steak is a feel thing; you've got to develop a sense of touch around the flesh of animals that becomes finetuned, accustomed to degrees of cooking. A good chef 'knows' when a fillet steak is medium well or medium rare or just on medium and they 'know' because they develop a sense of touch. By squeezing a steak while it cooks, a chef can develop an appreciation of what stage of cooking the meat is at. There's no quick and easy way to get to the point of consistently 'knowing', you just have to develop the skill.

One of the best ways to teach a chef how to cook a steak is to put it on the menu as a sliced dish. For instance the dish might read, *Sliced Angus tenderloin with yam puree and shitake mushroom jus*. Now the reason the tenderloin is sliced is because the chef, which in this case is me, is training an apprentice to cook steak. I want Jesse, Choc or Soda, or whoever it is in the next joint, to gain confidence in their ability to cook steaks by seeing and analysing the inside of every steak they prepare. So after they've seasoned the lump of beef with salt flakes and white pepper, and seared all the surfaces of the steak in their cast-iron pan, the fillet goes onto a clean tray and into the oven. Here's the other thing: every oven is different. Doesn't matter if Chef Pete puts it in for two minutes and Chef Jane says three and a half and Sous-Chef Donny goes six . . . Every steak and every oven is different, and the only way to get a steak medium rare, as the customer ordered it, is to be able to pinch the steak between your thumb and forefinger and know it's got a while longer in the oven or it's done. And done means it's ready to be rested. The steak needs to be transferred to your protein tray in a place where it is going to stop, or very quickly slow, cooking. It needs to be rested so that the blood can congeal or drain from the piece of meat before it gets plated up.

But before I let the apprentice slice the fillet, generally into three thick slices at a nice angle, we look at the steak, we touch the steak, we talk about the steak and watch as the blood soaks into the tea towel which sits on the protein tray. We slice the fillet and all agree that this is a perfectly cooked medium-rare fillet of beef and we discuss what it felt like when it came out of the oven— whose breast or bicep or thumb it most reminds them of. We do this because it's important to try to remember that touch. The steak is hot when it comes out of the oven and it always looks more cooked than it is because we've

seared it until the flesh has caramelised but the touch . . .
cooking steak to order is all about the touch.

After I'd been at the Bondi Hotel for some time, it
occurred to me that my twenty-first birthday was fast
approaching. It also struck me that despite the irrefutabil-
ity of time passing, I felt for the most part that I was in
some kind of holding pattern. Don't get me wrong, I was
happy there; it was a warm and cosy space. I was also in
some kind of prime-of-life, object-of-desire phase, and
the girls I was hanging out with didn't mind me stoned;
in fact, they seemed to like it.

I was sharing a flat up the road from the hotel in
Bennett Street. It was a nice top-floor apartment that
some boys from Canberra had rented and they were happy
for me to pay an equal share of the expenses and crash
in the sunroom. The view was all apartment building
rooftops and Bondi skyline. None of the boys in the flat
were attached to partners in any serious way, and other
than Paul, our resident gay nurse, we all worked at the
hotel. Sean had the bottle shop five days a week, Damian
pulled beers in the rooftop beer garden and Bruce . . .
I don't know what Bruce did, he just turned up for work.
Basically we lived like kings. And despite the boys getting
a little worried about my drug use after a year or so,
my twenty-first acted as a catalyst for us all to pool our
collective resources and organise a blast.

We decked the flat out in trippy fluorescent-tape wall
patterns and ultra-long-bongs. The bathtub was over-
flowing with the best the bottle shop had to offer and

we scored a veritable smorgasbord of drugs through our friends at the hotel—all of whom decided they weren't going to miss out on the action and turned up on the night. The flat was so crowded at one point that people literally couldn't move. Such was the interest in the party that I bumped into several undercover cops, a large variety of junkies from various surrounding suburbs and three different girlfriends from two different states. The Saints, the Smiths, the Velvet Underground, New Order's first album, Yello, the Pixies, Alien Sex Fiend, Johnny Cash and the Pogues . . . all were there in spirit if not in person, and I got so blissfully stoned with so many different people that—despite not really being able to focus on how Angela could actually be here from Brisbane while Marie from Paddington was wrapped under my right arm and Gayle from the hotel was giving me grief every time she caught sight of me—the night was a raging, police shut-down, music-ripping success. Except for some random bacteria that found its way into a syringe and blew up my groin in a way that was very far from normal. I didn't notice it until the morning after, and thankfully Paul had the good sense to get me to hospital, where I spent the next four days in a ward being lectured on how close I'd come to forsaking my capacity to father children.

Ward 4D was a window through which reality threatened to shine too brightly upon my youthful, hazy, drug-addicted ways. I did wake up to some things: I realised that, despite lying to the admissions doctors, I had become a self-injecting, poly-drug user; and I was drinking an amount of alcohol which sounded like a wild exaggeration when I admitted it to others. Yet I wasn't ready to consider giving up or cutting down on any of it. I'm sure I promised everyone that I would but, really, most of my so-called problems seemed like very distant concerns.

When I did get back to work, I started to pick up some shifts as a glassie after my shifts in the kitchen. Money was tight; I was young and the extra hours picking up empty schooner glasses off punters' tables didn't bother me. I figured I was going to be hanging around the place after work anyway, playing pool, smoking joints and drinking, I might as well be earning while I did so. Then I scored a solo shift in the drive-through and the thing about that was—and you have to remember this was pre-CCTV and pre-mobile phones, pre-internet and EFTPOS—being surrounded by an endless supply of bottles and cases of alcohol and cartons of cigarettes and a cash register which I was responsible for . . . well, it brought about a short sojourn out of the kitchen and into the world of being a drive-through attendant.

7

To be fair to Jesse, his parking run-in with the police was not completely unexpected. Parking at Watego's Beach during summer is a nightmare. And the particular skill set that finding a park entails deserves special mention. I know lots of places get busy over summer or winter or whatever the particular high season of that place is, but Watego's—a tiny suburb tucked in beneath the lighthouse on the most easterly point of Australia—is another thing altogether. We're on the very tip of things and while the vast majority of cars don't veer left off the road that leads up to the lighthouse in order to roll down into Watego's, those with the money or the longboards or the parking skills do, and enter what is a very particular kind of paradise.

Watego's is made up of about a hundred houses. All of them cost at least a few million dollars and some of them considerably more. It's not an ostentatious suburb to look at; in fact you hardly notice the houses for the blue-green sea, the dolphins, casuarinas and pandanus trees. The local council has graciously installed a couple of free barbeques beneath timber huts right on the beach-front and these are a great option for people—in winter. Winter is a great time to visit Watego's and Byron Bay generally. You can move around easily, park anywhere you want and fire up as many free barbeques as you like. Have all three barbeques for yourself if you like.

But I guess that's like going to the Snowy Mountains in summer—it's strictly for the bushwalkers. And I know bushwalkers are people too, but they usually prefer push-bikes to cars and strange amalgams of hydrated vegetable matter over a restaurant meal.

I swung left off Lighthouse Road this morning on my way to work and attempted to roll down the hill to Rae's; it was a fucking traffic snarl at nine o'clock in the morning! 'Don't you people have anything better to do?' I was yelling out my window. And of course they don't. They're all on holidays and are all determined to mark out their patch of sand on Watego's Beach. There will have been 'sitters' assigned to the barbeques by seven in the morning; no doubt for a child's birthday party or a fiftieth wedding anniversary or some random backpacker gathering.

As I crawled down the hill to Marine Parade I was greeted by about thirty vehicles backed up waiting for a park close to the beach. Anyone who walks up from the beach, even if they're only going for a shower, has sixty pairs of greedy eyes on them, tracking their every move.

To add pressure to proceedings, my wife Alice texted me a second picture of our two young boys fighting with each other. There was no message to accompany the image; she was relying on my ability to join the dots. After fifteen years together we can read each other's shorthand. This picture was designed to remind me that if I didn't work a million hours a week I would be home on New Year's Day helping her with the kids; at least to the extent that they would be hitting me rather than each other. Alice knows she can turn my car around with one softly spoken word; turn it around and have it never head back this way again. But right now, in the middle of this particular high season, we're both content to keep taking cheap shots at each other to alleviate the stress. There's a point where it isn't fun any more and people can get hurt, but for the moment we're just letting off a little steam.

Alice is disappointed that I'm not at home with the family today. Part of the deal with getting Christmas Day off was that I agreed to work every other day over the summer break—including New Year's Day. Really, she's seen it all before in regards to chefs and peak seasons and anyway, the photo of the kids fighting is just to remind me what it's like for her, having to deal with the boys by herself all summer. She needs to know that someone else can feel her pain.

Our eldest son is a full two years from going through puberty, but he's practising. It's a compelling performance. And it's a show that's been going on for about six months. As a team, we've recently surrendered to the idea that our children now have a speaking part in the small drama that constitutes our shared lives. Suddenly our kids are people too. None of the lines our boys are trialling are original nor are they anything we haven't heard before—it's just that we'd been suffering the delusion that only other parents had nightmare children.

Alice also understands completely that in order to meet the weekly demands of a modest mortgage, school fees and the running costs of two very second-hand cars, one of us has to work sixty to eighty hours a week somewhere, or we have to split the money-earning responsibilities and work around each other, juggling the kids as we go. We've tried both methods of family management and arrived at the conclusion that being young and irresponsible is grossly underrated.

Alice was twenty years old when we met. I was twenty-eight and sitting in a modest room above a suburban church. She walked in with a friend and within the first hour I knew I was studying my future bride. She was the opposite of me in nearly every way but I recognised her every look and mood. I knew why she glanced away or pulled at her hair or wriggled in her seat or coughed. I knew that the reason she glared intently at the boy sitting next to me was to deflect my love-struck grin.

From that first night it seemed clear to me that she possessed a particular kind of vulnerability that I was born to care for. There was—and is—something fierce and innocent about Alice. Normally I would have been more modest in my aspirations but there was this split second when she did return my stare and . . . that was all the time I needed. I was reborn, remade, recast and she quickly became the reason I breathed, woke up, caught the bus and went to work. In the story of my life, Alice has all the winning lines. As soon as I'd pictured us together, I became convinced that nothing bad could happen. And in the strangest of ways, I was right.

Not that she would have anything to do with me for the longest time. To suggest I was obsessive in those early days is an understatement. I was a badgering, hounding lunatic. And it wasn't until I convinced her to come out with me to a few decent restaurants that she glimpsed some faint potential. At an assortment of cafes, restaurants and wok-shops, I found the confidence to talk and act in a way that didn't mark me out as just a lunatic. I was a lunatic who could cook. And as the number of restaurants that we sampled grew, she began to allow me into other parts of her life. Sometimes she would let me pick her up from college. One red-letter day she took the risk of introducing me to some of her student friends, who I worked so hard at trying to charm that she desisted from any further such introductions for a long time. And yet I remained irrepressible: eager to lock things down, tie things up and throw away the key.

'I'm not ready to settle down,' she'd say. 'We're so young!'

It was a logic that was obvious to everyone but me. I was, apparently, tone deaf to the finer points of romance. But my life hadn't really unfolded in such a way that I could imagine how two people might go out on a few dates and have a little fun while they got to know each other. I seemed destined to always be the obsessive-compulsive smack-before-breakfast kind of guy who thought getting to know someone was the risk you took if you happened to wake up later than expected. ('Sorry . . . what was your name again?') And that wasn't the sort of thing Alice was up for.

Basically, I didn't know what fun looked like if it didn't come in the form of white powder—or beige or pink or brown or tar-coloured or . . . any colour of the rainbow.

Of course Alice has never forgiven me for winning out in the end. Our saving grace is that we did manage to spend five years together before the first of our two boys arrived. In retrospect we could have enjoyed a couple more. But what are you going to do?

As the third picture comes through on my phone I can sense that an actual call is not far off. She'll start by asking something like, 'Did you get the pictures?' And then follow up with some breaking news about not having any idea what to do with the kids day after day . . . without any money! And some time later, when the rest of the world's asleep, we'll wonder aloud how it all came to this and convince ourselves once more that, just like every other year, this high season will end too.

But this morning, like every other morning of high season, my most immediate concern was parking.

Off to the left, at Rae's, there's parking for about five of the guests' cars after Vinnie has lodged his Porsche sideways across the driveway. And while to roar down Marine Parade and screech up the paved drive at Rae's— which is the last strip of privately held real estate before the beach—is not everyone's idea of being a made man, for some it's a particularly sweet fantasy.

As luck would have it this morning, my secret parking spot was not taken. It's a spot famous among the staff at Rae's, right outside Deke's house, which, if he's not entertaining, he doesn't mind you using. It's a real treat.

And it's morally uplifting to be able to park there this morning. And it's not that I hate tourists—tourists are my bread and butter; I'm nothing without their desire to wine and dine at Rae's—it's just that because everyone else in the neighbourhood is on holidays there is often a certain tension between the stressed-out, overly tired, heap-of-shit-car-driving chefs and the rest of the punters. Quite simply, they don't get it. And that's okay! I'm sure I'd be a fish out of water in their world.

And just like every other morning I've walked into the kitchen at Rae's, this morning it smelt of sour cooking oil, cigarette smoke and bacon and eggs. Vinnie has been and gone—even though the Porsche was still in the driveway—having cooked breakfast for the guests who ordered it. Vinnie chooses to cook the breakfasts himself for two reasons: first, he hates paying a breakfast chef to do something that he considers unworthy of paid labour; and second, it's an ideal cure for a hangover. Same as every other morning Vinnie cooks breakfast, this morning the kitchen is a fucking mess.

I've had the privilege of doing a number of services in the kitchen with Vinnie Rae as head chef. And while publicly he taught me everything I know—when what I do is good—he's not what most people would call an organised or well-prepared chef. And that's because he doesn't have to be; when you own the joint, you can do what you like and I get that. It's just that sometimes it would be nice to walk in and not have to start cleaning up burnt toast and cooked egg whites and dirty pans. And the reason I have to start cleaning up rather than a kitchen hand or an apprentice is because he won't pay for them to start early.

Vinnie is big on wage control. He doesn't give a fuck about food costs, really—he's happy for the punters who pay the bills to have the best—but wages, forget about it. Every hour that a staff member works is akin to having them reach into his front pocket and pull out his money. It's an affront to him that people expect to get paid. After everything he's done for them! Not that anyone ever figures out what it is Vinnie actually has done for them, but that's beside the point; while you're scratching your head, he'll be in the surf dropping in on overweight tourists on rented McTavish mini-mals.

Scotty was in the house early this morning and that was comforting. Even if he was in a mild panic and rambling on about the carnage of last night which, as far as New Year's Eves go, was apparently a show-stopper. All of which I missed because I fled home straight after service. Scotty told the usual stories about celebrities and broken glass out by the pool. Broken bottles and broken vows and broken dreams and massive bills—that about covers the early morning gossip among the staff at Rae's before service begins. Out by the pool . . . I swear that space is a late-night fantasyland of fame and glory and money and models and champagne and—well, you can just picture the redemptive yoga practice come brunch time.

There's a barbeque next to the pool area that some-times inspires guests to borrow a chef from the kitchen and—with the smallest amount of help—throw together a rustic seafood lunch or some late-night Wagyu beef burgers. And maybe it's because everyone cooks at some stage of their life that some guests feel compelled to share a few of their greatest hits and memories in regards to all things cooking. Some of the tips are pure gold, really . . . It's not all bad, though. Over the past couple of years I've ended up cooking for Baz and CM a few times, dozens of models and various celebrities from around the globe. The people who can sit back, relax and enjoy the service seem to have the best time, whereas the guys who insist on showing the chef a thing or two invariably end up splattered with pork fat and chowing down on burnt beef. Go figure.

But then, just to shake things up this morning, Vinnie suddenly appeared at the bar, which is open at chest level through to the kitchen, dripping wet and smoking a fag.

'Chef! What's happening? You on top of it?' he shouted, blowing smoke into the kitchen as he set about making a juice in the bar blender.

'Yes, Vinnie,' I replied, a little surprised that he'd hung around after breakfast. 'We should be okay. Big night last night but I'll get the boys to hit the ground running. How was the surf?'

But Vinnie didn't want to talk about the surf. Other than as something for others to envy. 'You know me, mate, if it's big I'm out. It's all about the *mise en place* today, Jimmy, all right? Get fucking prepped up—and don't let that little Choc prick keep disappearing out the back gate.'

'What's he doing out there?' I asked.

'Oh, c'mon, he's a fucking pothead. He came walking back from the coolroom last night right when there were guests coming out of the toilets and he fucking reeked of dope. It's not a good look, mate.'

'I'll talk to him, Vinnie.'

'And make sure you get the boys to pick those crabs, all right? Get them on the menu for lunch.'

'Yes, Chef.'

'Have you done the lunch menu yet?' Vinnie asked, like he wasn't actually taking the piss.

'No, Chef. Scotty's not ready yet,' I lied, also taking the piss.

'Yeah, yeah. Scotty, why aren't you fucking ready, mate? It's fucking New Year's Day,' Vinnie yelled to Scotty, who was out in the restaurant area setting up tables.

Scotty started mumbling something from out on the floor but Vinnie just turned away, laughing. 'Silly cunt. Can't hear a word he's saying. And fucking clean this place up, all right, Jimmy?'

I shot him a look, like, *go easy*.

'Yeah!' Vinnie fired right back. 'I know it's busy, mate, but that's no excuse. You had the kitchen hand do fifty hours last week. He's taking home more than me.'

'Well, that means he's getting twice what I get and I did ninety hours,' I said, starting to get pissed off.

'Don't be a smart-arse, Jimmy, it doesn't suit you. And the boxes down in the garage, mate—what the fuck's going on down there?'

By now the blender in the bar was going full-blast as Vinnie leant into the kitchen blowing smoke everywhere and shooting down early morning flies with an aerosol can of Mortein.

'Jesus, Vinnie. Go easy on that stuff,' I warned as I loaded his dirty breakfast pans into the sink.

'You've got to do it early, Chef, give it a good spray before you start prepping, all right?'

'Yes, Chef.' I was starting to warm up.

'And get that little Soda cunt to flatten the boxes out, all right?'

'Yes, Chef,' I repeated, a little louder.

'And Jimmy,' Vinnie added as he floated past slurping on his juice, 'don't be a smart-arse, all right?'

'Yes, Chef!' I bellowed. And that's all he'd wanted to do. Get me fired up before the rest of the staff walked into the joint so they'd see me running rather than just warming up.

And as the 911 roared to life out in the driveway, its canvas roof folding back into its position behind the rear seats, I strolled out to the restaurant and kung-fu'd the air and side-kicked the flies. It was enough to make Scotty look up for a beat from his screaming vacuum cleaner and flick me a middle finger. And if it were any other day I would have gone on with it . . . but it's not, and I didn't. Instead I slapped my face a couple of times, sucked it up, and marched out to the coolroom, the familiarity of its smell already somewhere deep inside me.

8

A random stocktake at the Bondi Hotel brought my cosy world undone. Frankly, I had disappointed myself—and, more significantly, the general manager—during my time punching in numbers on the cash register in the drive-through. We shared a first name and he seemed to genuinely like me but when he sat me down one morning and said he had to let me go because the inventory was so many dollars out, the numbers shocked me. I protested, of course, but who else could he blame? I had the keys to the cash register and the coolroom; I refilled the cigarette shelves and replaced the bottles of wine. It's just that, until the three-monthly stocktake rolled around, I was in a space which might fairly be described as heaven on earth. Bondi in spring is a glorious thing: I always had cash in my pockets and a spare cigarette for the bums down the laneway where the drive-through operated at the back of the hotel; I was a trusted and even well-liked employee . . . and yet I was living a double life.

My heroin habit had become more concentrated after my stint in hospital. I let the late-night partying slide and slipped into the daylight gig of being a drive-through attendant. JD did the business of scoring for me, which kept the supply side of things comfortably mysterious. It just seemed a matter of convenience that he dropped by at the same time each morning and laid a deal on me. I was enjoying my time out of the kitchen. Life seemed easier, less dirty and hot, more colour and movement. And my time in the drive-through, while not profitable for the hotel, allowed me to reflect on what it meant to be a chef. And that reflection was brought about partly because everyone around the hotel still referred me as 'Chef'; it was like the job of cooking had named me and no matter how much I might want to fuck with my identity, people seemed to know me better than I knew myself: like, *of course you're a chef Jimmy, that's what you were always going to be—and what's wrong with that?*

After my meeting at the hotel with Big Jim I was feeling particularly low and decided to go see my mother. No biggie, give her a call and catch up, maybe tick her up for some cash and family news. As soon as I rang, though, I knew it was a mistake. Her first line was something like . . .

'You're never gonna guess what's happened to me!'

And naturally she wasn't interested in hearing anything from me except, 'What's happened to you, Mumma?' As if she couldn't actually conceive that I would be anything less than fascinated by what was going on in her life.

Which was the same old story: some rich client had fallen for her and was going to take her away from all this.

The capacity of my mother and some other women I've known to lay themselves down at the foot of some romantic dream of Prince Charming riding up and carrying them away—well, fuck me if it's not the most amazing thing. And it's like the dream never ended for my mother; like she was always and forever just some little girl biding her time and one day . . . one day *he* was going to crash through that door and carry her away. And of course at the brothel, they did that seven nights of the week.

So I trotted up to Bondi Junction, where she'd suggested we meet—just for a minute, mind, and no scenes, please. I sat down with the ladies to morning tea. Annie, the madam of the joint, was all professional sweetness and light. 'Hello, darling, how are you?'

The others joined in.

'Look girls, a famous young chef.'

'Keep your hands off, ladies, I saw him first.'

I have to admit, I was a sucker for it. And let's be clear: this was no teenage junkie ho club; this was in the 'top class' category of working ladies—and if you could get past the multiple oxymorons and sheer theatricality of the place, well . . . maybe you were never meant to do that anyway. It was instantly clear to me that problems did not exist here; this was a space of dreams and fantasy, a perfect world where a man could take a scotch on ice at the bar and nibble on some cashews while a bevy of scantily clad and adoring females satisfied his every need. A gentle shoulder massage, a giggle at his every word— truly, life had never been quite this grand.

But of course no one wants to see their mother at this point in the story.

'I'm not here for the candy, ladies.'

Giggle, giggle.

'I just need a little cash and to check up on my mum.'

Soothing massage.

'Back up now, girls. Give a man some breathing space.'

And with a departing scrape of fingernails on skin and a flicking of hair, they did. In this darkened room with its warm soft lights and faint piano, the temperature set to make you want to loosen your tie, every man was king as long as he paid. And really, that's the deal. What you're paying for in places like that is not really the sex; obviously that's the money shot, but the reason some places charge a hundred dollars an hour and others, like this one, five hundred, rests with their capacity to make a man feel like a king. In this world, the man is an all-powerful, all-knowing, wise and wonderful provider and expert lover. And there's no shortage of just-rich-enough cabbies prepared to pay for that illusion.

There was something about my mother that was not cut out to survive in the everyday world. And while it hurt me to see the way she deluded herself with impossibly romantic notions, I got so used to seeing her broken that I found I couldn't be angry with her after a while. I just came to accept that she probably wasn't going to change that much and, if I wanted to spend time with her at all, I would have to accept her the way she was.

My mother had six children and she loved us all. I was her second-born son and I was always close to her when I was a kid. I was fourteen years old when my parents divorced. It didn't particularly bother me when she ended up working as a hooker. It was more like the culmination of who she was rather than a desperate decision. If anything, it was something of a miracle that she'd managed to raise six kids at all.

Organising my first job for me at Oliver's in Townsville was her way of setting me up for the future. And she was serious about it. She didn't want me to fail: she was always talking me up and pushing me into things. But she was never so much a mother as someone to confide in. And while those conversations were becoming less frequent the older I got, there was nothing I wouldn't have done to make the world a better place for her. Fortunately, she felt the same way about me, and on this particular visit to the brothel she gave me a pile of cash.

When Annie and the other girls caught on that there wasn't going to be any great scene between my mother and me—that after a catch-up on family gossip and a few drinks we would simply go our separate ways—they let slip their various masks and alter egos and for a time became who they really were. No one was kidding themselves that life was perfect or that any one of us had woken up as kids and dreamt that this was the life we were going to lead, but the need for everyone to bullshit everyone else wasn't an issue.

The wind tunnel that is Bondi Junction seemed a little more bitter than usual that day as I walked away from the brothel and back towards the train station. I wondered at the time how it was all going to end. How was it possible that, after a few years of working at the Bondi Hotel, all I had to show for myself was a fistful of cash from my mother and a very demanding heroin addiction? I fantasised about drug runs to Thailand and dealing smack or growing pot and then, instead of doing anything so sensible, I raced down the escalator and jumped aboard a train to Kings Cross.

It was my mother who suggested I try a place in Balmain called Sorrentino's. She knew someone who knew something and I caught a bus across the harbour and liked what I saw. Balmain has more hotels per capita than just about anywhere else on earth.

The sun shone differently in Balmain: like it was outback rather than coastal, tree change rather than sea change. There was plenty of money around but it wasn't uptight—more creative than *Rich Dad, Poor Dad*. You could bump into semi-retired rock stars, film directors or painter-dash-sculptors who might sell pots for five grand rather than fifty cents at the Saturday market. In the late eighties it had that lazy, everyone's-a-home-owner kind of feel, which was nice given that I wasn't old enough to care I wasn't one of them. It never occurred to me that I should save any money or invest or indeed do anything other than work just hard enough to meet my most pressing needs.

The job at Sorrentino's was cold larder, which wasn't

glamorous, but I was happy enough without the pressure of being in front of the stove. I was actually determined to clean up my act and get a proper job again, a job in a big enough kitchen where I could learn some shit and fit in with a crew. And the crew at Sorrentino's were great but old. This was general Italian food rather than regional cuisine; a trattoria rather than fine dining. But it was busy and well liked and had been there for a long time, so it had that lived-in feel which I always like in a place. If a restaurant's too new I struggle to trust it somehow, as if they haven't worked out who they are yet. This joint was under no illusions.

I worked with two head chefs during my time at Sorrentino's. They were both good cooks and painted a picture for me about what was possible in a future of some kind. These guys were journeymen; they'd been cooking forever and were able, after negotiating what seemed like a huge salary, to walk into the kitchen and start work and by dinner time have everyone singing their praises. These guys weren't experimenting and they weren't surprised by a 'compliments to the chef'; they were playing a familiar tune which had worked in the last place they cooked or maybe it was a couple of places ago. They knew what their strengths were and how much they were worth. And both of them showed me a few tricks without finding the need to turn into any great mentor.

Doug, the owner of Sorrentino's, was better to me than he had to be. I don't know if he'd been told about any personal problems I was struggling with or if it was just in his nature, but as an owner he seemed to have complete faith that I would and could succeed as a chef.

He didn't let me near anything I was likely to rip off and wouldn't tolerate me coming in late. This was fine by me. I needed the weekly wage just to stay afloat. Life aboard the gravy train had ended after Bondi.

My biggest problem was that when I got straight or even semi-straight, I entered into some sort of reality I wasn't prepared for. At times life seemed illogically hard and physically painful even. Muscle aches and pains, stiff joints and lethargy . . . Sometimes I'd look at myself in the mirror and go, *dude, you are a young man, what the fuck is the problem here?* And because I never got straight long enough to properly detox, and because I never managed to give everything up, just swapping the witch for the bitch, it seemed only logical that I would end up self-medicating with heroin again whereupon, like magic, I would feel 'normal'. But because I'd left Bondi and JD behind, I had to score for myself, and that meant catching a bus or a train up to Kings Cross and dealing with the street hustlers. Which I didn't really mind, it's just that it took a few hours to do that from Balmain and Doug wasn't the sort of boss who liked to give me a whole lot of time off. So my drug using at that point became an every-few-days affair. On those days I didn't go up to the Golden Mile, I simply smoked some grass and got smashed on cheap wine and good whisky.

Then, one day, Doug offered me the deal of a lifetime.

Doug was a businessman, he wasn't a cook, and he only really acted at being a host. This is not to say he didn't enjoy it. Shit, I think he was having the time of his life. He'd bought the restaurant as a very going concern and was able to hang about the place doing deals with suppliers, hiring and firing staff, and generally keeping on top of the paperwork while he sucked back the *vino rosso* and called for more cheese. And he did it well. But he was always looking to expand and even franchise the restaurant concept—which is never a good idea. Outside of fast food, I don't think franchising works. I know some place, somewhere, will prove me wrong, but I probably wouldn't rate the joint anyway.

So Doug did what every ambitious restaurateur does and took on some partners. The Italians, as they became known, were a couple of entrepreneurs who had imported all the necessary machinery from Italy to make commercial quantities of fresh pasta. And they were good, hard-working Italian boys rather than dreamers or mafioso. They already had some successful fresh pasta 'huts' in shopping centres and the plan was to bring a trattoria dining experience—like Sorrentino's—into the fresh pasta 'huts' and generally take it all to the next level. So they opened in some pretty exposed public places, and soon the Balmain version of things got rubbed with the Circular Quay version of things, which brought the whole experience of dining at 'a' Sorrentino's down to the lowest level. It wasn't like you could have one flagship restaurant that was somehow superior to the others; people ate at or saw the other version of things and that's what they started to equate with Sorrentino's.

The thing about the pasta machine of the Italians was that it was capable of pumping out a lot more pasta than they were able to sell. They'd opened a place in King Street, Newtown, which in the mid-eighties was a particularly grungy part of what was predominantly a university suburb in the inner west of Sydney, and the shop went belly up. The fit-out was good—they had put in quality equipment and signed a long lease—but after about six months they were losing so much money they decided they were better off with the place closed. So they offered it to me.

Basically the deal was that I walk into the joint, open it up under whatever name I wanted, pay the rent, and they would give me a three-month supply of as much fresh pasta and sauces as I needed. The rent was next to nothing; it was a bargain. I could see right away that the problem with the place was that the branding was too conservative for its location. It was out of place in what was a lowbrow, drug-fuelled, rock-and-roll neighbourhood. It was a hundred metres up the road from the Sandringham Hotel, which at the time was one of the premier performing spaces for alternative music. It was a hip part of town before it got hip . . . but you could feel it coming. The problem was that not enough people were walking down the street at the right time of day—but if you were twenty-two and had your ear to the ground, you could hear the traffic coming. And I jumped at the chance.

10

It's not unusual for chefs to use a whole lot of drugs, drink like alcoholics and smoke a pack a day. Commercial kitchens are the last bastions of *I don't give a fuck* when it comes to the random, hedonistic consumption of legal and illegal intoxicants. And because chefs work so many hours over such a broad sweep of the week, particularly during times when others are letting their hair down, most chefs see it as their responsibility to roster on having a few beverages or joints or lines during work hours. And I'm fine with that; I don't do it myself any more, but I'm hardly in a position to instruct others not to. Which is just as well because Choc, who Vinnie spoke to me about earlier in the day, has disappeared for longer than his requested two-minute piss-break.

There was the briefest of lulls in the kitchen ten minutes ago and Choc, sensing an opportunity, grabbed his balls and pointed to the bathrooms.

'Two minutes,' I yelled after him as he walked out of the kitchen, past the bar and down the tunnel towards the toilets. The problem is that beyond the toilets and the coolroom and the pool there is a gate that opens onto a small patch of bushland. And for Choc, there are mermaids singing out there. It's a quiet and damp and silent place where a weary chef or a bush turkey might rest awhile before rejoining the madness that exists inside Rae's rendered pink walls.

Jesse has moved his car and is talking in hushed tones to Soda about what the police told him. Byron Bay is a small town, so if you happen to meet the police at some point, you quickly become known to them. Both Soda and Jesse are on first-name terms with most of the officers.

'Did they let you keep the keys, Jesse?' I enquire.

'Yes, Chef. Everything's all right. They just wanted me to move the car.'

'Where did you get a park?'

'Got the glory park right out front, Chef.' Jesse smiles.

'Lucky,' I reply. 'Listen, I'm going to go drag Choc back inside. You two clear the dishes off the waiters' station and make a little bench space. You're about to get smashed with the rest of the dessert orders.'

'Yes, Chef,' they chorus, getting on with the job straight away.

Jesse and Soda are more animated than they have been for days and no doubt it's because they can sense an impending drama that involves the law. Whatever they're up to—and I really would prefer not to know—will require me to try to limit the fallout. And I must do this if I am going to physically survive the next few days because I simply cannot have one of them not turn up to work.

The irony of me being, in the boys' eyes, the old straight dude down by the stove who couldn't possibly understand the extent of their debauchery and evil ways . . . well, it's bittersweet. I certainly never planned to be that guy. In fact my whole life can probably be described as a failure to plan, but time gets away from us all.

Walking from the kitchen out to the coolroom at Rae's requires walking through the back of the restaurant. It's something I haven't had to do during lunch service today, and it's refreshing to see all the guests having a good time. You can sometimes forget that people are relaxing and enjoying themselves just a few metres from where you're stressing out and fending off chaos. Paris and Nicky and the rest of the girls at their table seem to be genuinely happy as they finish up their desserts. The two security guys, who are sitting at a table next to the girls, shoot me a wink and half raise their beer glasses. Scotty is hovering, picking off empty glasses and finished plates. The sun is arching back somewhere overhead, its fierceness giving way to afternoon shadows.

Out beyond the pool, through the back gate, Choc is sitting on a log staring foggy-eyed at a water dragon.

'Hey, mate,' I call, breaking his spell.

'Oh, hey, Chef.' Choc quickly stubs out his joint.

'Listen, I just thought you should know that Vinnie is pissed off about you coming out here and sparking up. He's talking about putting a lock on the door so no one can use it.'

'Oh, no way!' replies Choc, who sounds eager to be neither the guy who screws up everyone else's good time, or inappropriate with me, his head chef—the tension of which forces a stoner's giggle out of him.

'Mate, I need you to keep your shit together until Thursday. You've got two days off then and you can have a blow-out, okay?'

'Yes, Chef. Sorry, Chef.' Choc sounds overly serious as he gets up off his log and walks back past me into the pool area.

'Don't be sorry, Choc. Just pace yourself and we'll be through the worst of the high season in no time, all right?'

'Yes, Chef.' He strides back into the kitchen.

And it is nice out here in the damp undergrowth, where I wait a moment and breathe in the moist air that still has traces of Choc's dope floating around. It's a little plot of nature that has survived the crush of sports cars and sunscreen, the longboards and the hot open beach. And the smell of the joint has me sucking in a few extra deep breaths. But while I'd truly love a joint right now, or a couple of beers or a bottle of something red, I know that getting pissed or stoned at this point in the game is going to send me to a place I won't readily be able to escape from.

I take out my phone and flick back through the photos Alice sent me earlier in the day. There are two new pictures, which are of plants throwing off new shoots from previously pruned branches. Alice has taken up gardening in the last year or so with something of a born-again fervour. The plants are slowly learning who's boss.

I snap a picture of myself, careful to get as much of my blood-, sauce- and fat-splattered tunic in the frame as I can, and send if off with a *Day off tomorrow!* message.

Back in the kitchen Jesse and Soda are semi-organised, which is novel. They have smashed through about twenty loads of dishes and cleared off the larder bench in order to set up the pastry section *mise en place*. The dessert orders are racking up on their docket clip and they are communicating: this is progress; this is good. Watching these guys take some responsibility, call the pass and clap the food out, is motivating. It means I can now fill a bucket of soapy water and start scrubbing down my section. I begin by piling all the dirty pots and pans onto the floor in the galley. I can't afford to slow down yet or stop moving for fear that my knees will seize. It's not a joke, I'm afraid. And I'm not that old. I'm a good four to eight years younger than Vinnie, depending on how old Vinnie is this week, and I should be fitter. My muscles and joints should be more agile and supple. But like I said, the life of a chef is physically demanding and the longer it goes on the more I realise I will have to start implementing strategies to cope with future high seasons.

During the quieter times I'm fine, no problem, king of the world. Come schoolies week, though—that faintly ridiculous tradition where the kids who've completed high school all pour out from the cities and hit the party towns up and down the east coast—I know it's time to get the yoga mat out of the cupboard and start making a fool of myself in the sanctity of my bedroom. It's a lonely experience, my yoga practice, which, as a ritual,

71

has all the visual appeal of an angry, overweight, mid-life contortionist rather than the elegant flow of Salutations to the Sun and Legs up the Wall in Bhujangasana.

'Jesse, what petits fours have you got?' Scotty barks into the kitchen.

'Chocolates,' Jesse answers.

'That's it?' Scotty demands.

'Fifteen years . . .' I start mimicking Vinnie.

'It's been an unbroken chain for fifteen years until you got here, Jesse,' Scotty finishes.

'Unbroken, strong!' I add.

'Yeah, yeah, whatever,' Jesse says wearily, like he doesn't give a fuck.

'You turn up at Rae's and the fucking petit four chain breaks,' Scotty continues in perfect Vinnie-speak as he scrapes off dirty plates and stacks them, ever higher, in the waiters' station.

'We haven't run out—there's chocolates,' Soda chimes in.

'Well, get the fucking things,' Scotty tells them. 'The girls are having a coffee and then they're going. They want to be out in fifteen minutes.'

And as Scotty disappears from the kitchen, you can sense his frustration at not having raised Vinnie on the phone. And it is unusual that Vinnie hasn't answered his mobile all day. His timing is usually impeccable, turning up at the exact moment someone starts mimicking him or just as a chef sits down to eat something after fifteen hours on their feet. And when he does arrive, right at the moment Scotty raises a beer to his lips, just after the restaurant has cleared out, he'll immediately start pointing out everything that's wrong with the restaurant by ringing out a list of all the things that need to happen—now! Vinnie knows the danger of tired bodies slowing down. It's like all he ever sees is the lack of value in someone moving at anything less than his or her most efficient speed. For Vinnie, anything other than intense focus and complete application is a cop out and it shouldn't matter that you've just worked a triple shift non-stop. That level of commitment can be very inspiring. And it's in demanding nothing less than the very best from his staff that Vinnie is able to maintain the lifestyle he has become accustomed to.

Soda passes the handmade chocolates through to the bar, where Sammy the barman ferrets them away into the back of the wine fridge. The petits fours are the equivalent of gold in the bar, particularly during the high season when the time it takes chefs to set the chocolate moulds, make the fillings and pour the casings is time that could be spent on a whole lot more pressing things.

11

I was excited at the start of the Pasta Man. The idea of being my own boss, working my own hours and reaping whatever rewards I could from my efforts was something I was eager to set in train.

Initially I spent hours just hanging around inside the shop with the lights out, working out what I was going to do with the space. There were limitations; I had to work with the existing equipment but that was all top quality anyhow. I began to see what colours might work and how a blackboard menu could function. This wasn't a restaurant; it was a cafe with a coffee machine and fresh pasta for sale as well as cooked pasta meals in a separate heated bain-marie.

It was the time of *Interview* magazine and I had a subscription because I thought it was about the coolest thing on Planet Earth. I got to cutting out pictures and pasting them up on the walls, drawing inspiration from its photographs and from the busy street outside. There was a seat out front which I painted the same colours as the shop to bring something from the outside in. I employed an Italian girl who was going to university and lived down the road. She was an artist and good with colours and ideas and people and . . . like me, not so good with drugs. But in the early days, I didn't care about that. This was the opportunity I had been waiting for and I was determined to make each step a winner by taking everything I knew about hospitality and pouring it into this space.

Opening night was a fucking killer. I haven't opened anything more than a tub of yoghurt since because it would have to be the most nerve-racking thing imaginable. And another thing, because the place had a counter, I was always in contact with customers. If everyone's got their strengths and weaknesses, talking to people about the same stuff over and over again was never one of my strong points. But it was all money, and from day one things were going pretty well. People were walking into the shop and spending cash; that was good, that was action. Almost immediately, the business was doing better than its previous incarnation, which made Doug and the Italians happy. They were dishing up free pasta, after all, so the place was still costing them money, but from week one there was enough turnover to pay the rent, the bills and me. I couldn't really do the maths on what it was going to cost to actually buy the produce from the Italians when the three months was up, but no one else seemed to be worrying about that either.

I had a flat above Rockefeller Bar & Grill in Darling-hurst and used to scooter to work over in Newtown each day. It was about a five-kilometre trip through peak-hour traffic but I was happy to commute because I liked living near Kings Cross and the nightclubs. When I'd come home from work around nine o'clock, I'd go have a few beers and catch a band, or sometimes get a little more wasted, but I felt positive about the business and life in general—like I had some control over what was happening.

In week three of running the Pasta Man my scooter got stolen, and that was truly fucked because I didn't have the money to buy a new one and I had to catch public transport, which added two hours to each day I worked.

After about four weeks, I realised I couldn't continue doing seven days a week, fourteen hours a day. The old Greek couple down the road did it; hell, they'd probably done it their whole lives, but frankly the picture they cut wasn't how I saw my future. So I did what any business-man does who wants to expand—in this instance into some more free time—and took on a partner. Who was also a friend. And it went well for a while. He wasn't a chef but you didn't have to be to do what we were doing, which was basically cooking off fresh pasta and heating up sauce, adding some vegetables and herbs, and then serving it out of a bain-marie. Like I said, it wasn't fine dining but we also brought some love to the food. It wasn't just a squat and gobble; we used to light some candles and put on some nice music and turn the lights down low at dinner . . . really, things could only get worse.

Pretty soon I figured out how the local smack scene worked. These things are fluid and you need some time to tune into the street in the sense that, while you might see the same dealer on the same corner a few days in a row, only a fool would rush in, particularly a fool who was now a visible part of the local business scene. We had regular customers and suppliers, and people I waved to each morning. And if people noticed me getting on with Paddy at the train station, that would not be good for business.

Eventually I was able to work out a plan with Chris, the local dealer, who was mad, bad and entirely dangerous. Basically he would send someone by the shop at the same time each morning, someone different, mix the faces up, and I would pay them while they had a coffee on the house. You didn't want someone running in and out, you wanted an invisible scene, something no one else would notice, because what had become apparent to me over the last couple of years was that being a junkie didn't make anyone Mr Popular. People were actually quite down on my comrades in the smack world, and while that was depressing for those of us on the inside, it was never reason enough to stop chasing another rabbit down a hole.

There was a very busy hairdressing salon next door and one of the guys, Terry, used to drop by and fix up with me. He was about ten years older and was very down on himself about using.

'Dude,' I would say, concerned about how upset he was getting, 'just don't do it.'

And Terry used to smile as he wrapped the belt tighter around his arm, searching desperately for a vein that had any courage, before he'd put his shot away and tell me not to worry.

'It's okay,' he'd say. 'Everything's going to be fine.'

And I was like, 'I know that, man.'

'You're younger than me,' Terry would say. 'You'll understand in a few years.'

'I won't be using in a few years.'

'Sure you won't,' he'd say, and smile. 'I won't be either. Right?'

'Yeah, right.'

I was surprised that people who used smack always felt like they couldn't stop, that they had no control. I'd heard the rumours before I started of course, and maybe that was what attracted me in the first place: the idea that a drug could be so powerful that you had no control over whether or not to get the next shot. It seemed like a challenge in some ways, like the ultimate game of truth or dare.

I'd watch Terry the Hairdresser walk back outside onto busy King Street after his shot, and he'd be strutting, like now everything was okay. He'd be smiling and waving to his customers, his face held to the sun. And in those brief moments of euphoria, Terry was Mr Respectable. He was Mr Fucking Hollywood Hairdresser. Everything came together for him over the next ten minutes or half-hour or even hour, if he was lucky. And then some broader reality would start to creep in, like an anxious snake in the veins, and it wasn't just a psychological thing, it was physical; the body would begin talking and what it started saying was, *you really need to start thinking about the next shot* now *or these worms of discontent are going to eat away at you from the inside out.*

12

Alice sends through a photo of an old couple deep in conversation on a park bench. It's an ironic scene. Alice is a people person. She needs to spend a set number of hours with adults in order to feel connected to the world. It's hardly too much to ask for. Part of the problem with living in Byron Bay at this time of year is that most of the locals have left town for somewhere quiet. And they leave because the cafes, streets and shops become overrun with backpackers and tourists.

Simple things like shopping for groceries require strategic planning and a commando's precision. Given the kids don't really understand the finer points of such missions, stress builds to the point where it becomes easier not to go into town at all. Soon—because your friends who don't work in hospitality have all departed—a sort of suburban isolation sets in which quickly becomes all-encompassing, like an endless stretch of time in which nothing seems to change.

Alice's recent obsession with the garden is in part inspired by the desire to witness change. It's like the miracle of watching a fern or shrub spring back from a particularly brutal pruning serves as proof that life is not a stagnant thing but a process of constant metamorphosis.

Two weeks ago, Alice turned up at work unannounced with the kids trailing along behind her. Our kids like Rae's; they've become familiar with the building's hidden spaces and comfortable curves. They know intimately, like children do, the most comfortable places to fold into and stretch out on. And I like to encourage such confidence and familiarity—in winter. Alice was aware that turning up with the kids just as lunch service began was going to throw Vinnie, me and the restaurant out; that's exactly what she planned to do. So aggrieved had she become at not spending any time together as a family that she decided it was time to make a statement.

Vinnie immediately ordered the kids some fries with tomato sauce and Alice a flat white, all the while berating me for not spending more time with my family. 'Jesus, Jimmy, are you still here? Will somebody tell this bloke that the place is capable of running without him for a couple of days?'

Then, in a fuck-you to the already overworked chefs, he loaded up a plate of very time-consuming-to-prepare petits fours for the kids to munch on while they waited for their fries. 'Are you going down for a swim, Alice? Do you need some sunscreen for the kids? Some towels? Just grab them from reception.'

'Thanks, Vinnie.' Alice smiled, playing along. 'We're fine. We won't be long. The boys just wanted to see their father.'

'Of course they do,' Vinnie said, full of indignation, like *how could you abandon your own children, Jimmy?*

'They haven't seen him at all this week,' Alice added, her voice slightly high-pitched.

'I've told him,' Vinnie said, shaking his head.

And Alice knows—because I've told her after other such impromptu drop-ins—that while it might be a real gas for her and Vinnie to stand around for ten minutes banging on about how fucked I am, how I can't even organise the kitchen to the point where I might get a little time off, the price of such fun is, for me, more of the same.

'I keep telling him, love,' Vinnie said, as he personally delivered the fries to the boys, who were moulded around the freshly laundered linen on table four. 'Get your roster fixed up.'

Table four has the best seats in the house. It's the first table booked for whatever VIPs are around on any given day and, because Alice turned up at quarter to twelve, Scotty was now going to have to do a miraculous quick-change as soon as the boys finished their fries in order to reset it for lunch.

It's not that Alice is unaware that each time I follow Vinnie's sage advice and roster myself off for two or three consecutive days he reaches for the red pen and starts crossing out shifts where I've rostered on other chefs. Failing that, he'll sack someone or send the kitchen hand home early and the phone will ring and Vinnie will say something like, 'I'm not paying you a hundred grand a year to lie around on the fucking beach, mate.' And his tone of voice will be adding, *how fucking dare I think that's okay?*

The boys managed to smear the tablecloth with at least half the tomato sauce and quickly devoured the plate of petits fours . . . minus the biscuit crumbs on the floor and the chocolate fingerprints that patterned the chairs.

And suddenly the clock struck midday and the first of our lunch guests began arriving and Vinnie, with the slightest shrug of his shoulders, directed a look at me that said, *thanks for that, Jimmy; you've set everyone back fifteen minutes, the restaurant's a disgrace and your kids are now running around the hotel in their boardshorts and thongs looking for towels and sunscreen.*

Children are not catered for at Rae's. Really, call up the office and tell Marionne you want to spend thirteen hundred bucks a night in room one and, by the way, you've got a two-year-old.

'So sorry,' she'll murmur. 'We're all booked out that weekend.'

And that's because Rae's is a sexy place; a romantic getaway; a lover's nest. It's a place to have a blow-out, unwind and relax—to drink too much and sleep in and order room service for lunch.

Alice understands all this better than anyone. But the thing is I made certain promises to Alice when we met; things like not letting life get so busy that we ended up not spending any time together. They were promises that I was desperate to keep. Hospitality doesn't lend itself to happy families, though. It's the hours: breakfast, lunch and dinner. If a chef spends the vast majority of their time cooking those meals for other people there's a price to pay at home, where partners and kids are doing the same thing, all the while wondering what Dad, or Mum, is cooking for the guests at the restaurant.

We've talked so many times about opening our own place. But each time we go to put it together something happens which demands our time or focus or money or . . . maybe I just never wanted to anyway. After running the Pasta Man all those years ago, I got a strong sense of never again wanting to get trapped anywhere seven days a week. I liked the freedom of leaving a job and moving on. And I liked learning new cuisines and new menus, things I could never have dreamt up if I didn't work in a whole lot of different kitchens.

Johnnie was my new business partner at the Pasta Man. I'd met him a few years earlier in Queensland, where he'd run a spectacularly unsuccessful fashion business, and we'd clicked instantly, like old mates. And like me, he could see the opportunity that the Pasta Man represented. We organised to work four days a week each. There would be one day where we'd cross over and work together and the rest of the week we'd run our three days independently of each other. We had Rosemary, my Italian junkie princess from down the street, and Bruce, my old flatmate from the Bondi days, to help us out on our respective days.

And really, our biggest problem was me. I had control over the cash register and the casting vote on whether to pay bills or pay myself—and I just kept paying myself rather than the business. And while some entrepreneurs might believe that's exactly how you get rich, the problem with my model was that all the money went up my arm. Given we weren't yet paying the Italians for the pasta and bulk sauce they were providing us, the date when we had agreed to start paying was beginning to look like the end of good times and the return of me doing a whole lot more hours for a whole lot less money. So to avoid the issue altogether, I took to getting the most outrageous, most money-hungry, most desperate heroin habit to date. What the Pasta Man became after a couple of months in was my best opportunity yet to pinch as much money from a cash register as I could in order to get as fucked up as possible.

Implementing that business model was a great shame for everyone involved. Essentially, I squandered everyone's good intentions and ripped off the business and pissed it all up against the wall. Not all of it was bad. Like I said, using smack is not all downside; it gets a lot of negative PR out there in the mainstream press but the real problems only start when the money or supply side of things begin to get messy. The great 'white-lady dream' of any junkie is an unlimited supply; anyone who's been using for a while and had to deal with a few periods of enforced detoxification will tell you that if only they could manage to get the supply-and-demand cycle right, they wouldn't have any problems in life. Most junkies can function reasonably well in the real world if they have low-level jobs and little ambition. And the others are better off staying home with Mum.

Johnnie had his problems, as any individual does, but he also had a pregnant wife and a mortgage on a house around the corner. He had respectable friends who supported him, and us, in the business, and his refusal to engage with the numbers of the operation was only going to last for so long. Pretty soon we cut the cross-over day so that the routine became one three-day week followed by a four-day week, and we got to never seeing each other. He took control when he was rostered on and I did so when I was on. And that included doing the paperwork, which was increasingly becoming a fantasy-land of its own.

One particular low point at the Pasta Man came about as I was standing behind the fresh pasta counter. The noodles were displayed in attractive handmade wooden trays with golden semolina sprinkled over the various shapes to keep it soft. It was a display worthy of a David Jones food hall. And as I waited for an old girl to make her pasta selection, it became obvious she was stuck looking at me, like I presented some sort of barrier she couldn't overcome in order to indicate which pasta she wanted to purchase.

'I don't think I'll worry about it today,' she said, like she loved the pasta but I was the fucking problem. And then she just walked out.

So I turned to cop a look at myself in the mirror and saw what she saw. Here was a young guy with several cold sores around his mouth, skinny around the chops, and then there was the hair . . . Terry from next door had taken to doing my hair for a tickle, which is about half a shot, and he did it after closing time so we wouldn't be bothered while we got smashed and talked shit. No one wants to be the centre of attention when they're demonstrably off-chops—either cutting hair or getting their hair cut—and the thing is, he was probably a little more fucked up than either of us realised and the colour job, which was meant to be blue-black, had turned a little multicultural. There were shades and patches happening that would have got a first-year apprentice sacked, but at the time we didn't notice; we were both talking it up, we were rock-and-fucking-roll.

But later, in the Pasta Man, I had one of those rare and scary moments of insight, which went something like, *this is not going to end well.* So I immediately turned away from my reflection and denied what I had just seen. But my insight was strong; Old Testament commands came booming forth and I didn't want to listen to any of it but the words were erupting inside my mind and echoing around the room.

You don't look so good, friend.

You're broke, friend.

You're ugly and you stink.

You have really fucked this up and in about five minutes everyone is going to find out.

So I did what any self-respecting drug addict would have done and hung up the optimistically titled and jauntily fonted BACK IN FIVE MINUTES sign and hit the streets looking for a deal. And of course things are not inclined to go well for the desperate junkie. A more prudent, more seasoned campaigner might have whispered caution or wise words at this point, but I didn't give a fuck, and upon seeing Paddy at the train station I greeted him like he was my long-lost brother or old mate from primary school and he was like, *be cool, man,* but I wasn't cool; I was fucking desperate.

Because Paddy was a grade-one cunt he wanted to go on with the whole best-mate scenario for the benefit of the locals, who were constantly on the phone to the cops about him, reporting his every little move. Well, now he was going to show them all who was fucking boss.

'You need what, Jimmy?' Paddy asked, dumbstruck, as if in all the years he'd been in his line of work he'd never heard of such an outrageous request. He motioned me to sit down beside him on an old bench carved with graffiti.

'I can't do tick, maaaate. You know thaaaat.'

And he was sorry for me. He was genuinely fucking concerned, and you could hear it in his voice. If you listened really hard.

'I'm just across the road, Paddy. You know me, mate. You know I'm good for it.'

'Maaaate, I wish I could. I really fucking doooo.' Paddy went on one of those epic round-the-world-with-multiple-fucking-stopovers nose scratches. He missed his snog eight or nine times until eventually I lifted his wasted wrist to his face for him, more out of concern for what other people were thinking about me at this point than any particular care I had for his unscratched itch. And Paddy, who was so wonderfully and riotously stoned, so gloriously in the sun, on the nod, turned to look at me as I lifted his hand to his face and ended up getting one of his own fingers in his eye.

'What are you fucking doing?' Paddy yelled, standing up, making a scene.

'Sorry, mate. Fuck, are you all right?'

'No, I'm not all right, you fucking cunt. You took my eye out.'

'Paddy, show me, man. Show me your eye.'

'Fucking get away from me, you prick. You know I don't do tick. Don't come over here begging and crawling like some fucking tip-rat. I run a respectable business over here.' He walked away, holding his eye and shaking his head, like he couldn't believe what some people would do to get on.

The Newtown train station was a busy place. People were looking at me, obviously wondering what I'd done to upset Paddy. Paddy was a man who didn't do emotion. He stalked; he didn't chat and he didn't quibble. Paddy was the street hustler for the bad, mad and evil Chris, who I had now upset by proxy. And that wasn't good. Nothing was good. So I went to step two of what any self-respecting junkie who can't get on does, and jumped on a train to Kings Cross.

Up at the Cross I felt instantly better. Kings Cross is a place where it's okay to let it all hang out. And people do. Everywhere. It was just what I needed. There was only one major problem and that was I only had five dollars. Which didn't make me unique. There were dozens of people up and down the main street looking to get on without any money. But as I stepped onto the main drag on that particular sunny morning, I convinced myself I was the most desperate of them all.

I crossed the street, dodging traffic and scanning the crew, trying to make eye contact with one of the working girls who was dealing. And when our eyes met, there was the usual almost imperceptible nod, which indicated the shop was open. She played her part by turning away from me and walking in the opposite direction as I strolled up behind her. And as I fell into step with her, she took a balloon-covered cap from her mouth and held it out behind her. My part of the deal was to press a crisp fifty into her upturned palm . . . But I didn't do that: I pushed a folded five-dollar note into her fist, grabbed the cap, and ran.

'Hey!' she yelled.

And she continued to yell as I raced away. It was almost as if she thought I was unaware of the fact that I'd just ripped her off; as if I might have somehow mixed up all the notes in my pocket and pressed the purple one into her hand rather than the greenback. But there was no mistaking of notes. I'd just scammed her.

I was approaching my mid-twenties by then and I can only surmise that the human body is a very forgiving machine. That or I was just incredibly scared, because I was not just *a* cheetah but *the* Cheetah. I didn't live very far from Kings Cross and I could have stopped off at home, put the shot away, then caught a cab back to work using some loose change. Instead, I ran a couple of kilometres, until I was able to jump on a bus that was heading straight to Newtown, and then sat down rolling the greasy stolen cap between my sticky fingers.

And while my heart was pumping more blood through its valves than it had since high school, I was crippled with what might be called an over-responsible fever to get back to the shop and get it opened. The thing I felt most strongly in the madness of that . . . madness, was the shame of abandoning the Pasta Man. My sole ambition, now that I had a deal in my pocket, was to get back inside the familiarity of its *Interview*-pasted walls and serve the customers who needed fresh pasta for their dinner; serve the workers who needed lunch from the bain-marie; and serve the people to whom I owed a lot of money and considerable goodwill.

I hurried back into the shop and bolted the door shut behind me so that I could shoot up. I determined I would throw out the food in the bain-marie, get a pot of water on the stove for some fresh pasta, and maybe buy some flowers. I reached for the checked chef's cap and put it on my head, wiped my face down with some Wettex and then bit the balloon casing from the cap and poured the white powder into a dessert spoon. I sucked up fifty mils of water with a syringe, squirted it back into the spoon, stirred the powder and the water together with the butt of the syringe and drew it back up into the needle through a cigarette filter. I popped a vein, which were frankly fucking pumping after my mid-morning run, then put the stolen deal away.

As the smack flooded through my veins, I felt both intense relief and had a vision of how the shop was going to look in about twenty minutes, after I'd cooked off some new dishes, got some sweet music playing and bought those happy flowers.

When I woke up it was dark. My face was deeply grooved from lying on the cigarette packet and spoon. Outside, cars were tearing along King Street on their way home, and inside I was more alone than I had ever been.

14

Vinnie has sacked Scotty on three separate occasions over the last few years and today could well be number four if Scotty doesn't manage to contact him and let him know that Paris is in for lunch. And by sack I mean, 'Fuck off and don't come back.' And after each such occasion, Scotty has gone and got another job and moved on with his life. Then Vinnie employs a new maître d' and after about five minutes realises that no one else is quite like Scotty. The same problem always recurs for Vinnie—and always after a short period of time: the new maître d' begins thinking they actually run things out on the floor. This might be the job description of a maître d' in other restaurants, but at Rae's it is just seen as so much arrogance. And in Vinnie's eyes, arrogance is very unbecoming in a waiter. And maybe Scotty's not the best maître d' in the world, maybe he even pisses some customers off, but he does possess the rare skill of being able to put up with Vinnie's illogical ways of dealing with the world. And that unique quality means that he has become something of a hero at Rae's.

The money the maître d' gets paid in wages and tips is good; sometimes at Rae's it's even great, since the hotel occasionally attracts those super-rich folks for whom tipping can become a game of one-upmanship. Waiters go home and pray for those people to sit down at a table in their section. Literally, on their knees, prayers before bed. I've seen it. And maybe in Scotty's case he was doing something else while he was on his knees, but as I've always said to the guy, 'It's because you can do two things at once that Vinnie loves you, mate.'

During the high season Scotty's tips can total well over a thousand dollars a week. After you factor in his pitiful wages, he can almost afford to rent somewhere in town where, after a bruising day at the office, he can run a hot shower, shine his shoes and get ready to do it all over again. That's Scotty's dream for next year anyway, a place in town. Until then he's happy enough driving the fifty kilometres to work each day.

'Push those desserts out, Jesse,' I say as I slop water over the stainless-steel wall behind the stove.

'Yes, Chef,' Jesse replies, clapping twice and calling, 'Service!'

'Those fucking waves are calling me, you hear?'

'You heading out, Chef?' Soda asks.

'You're damn right I'm heading out, Sodapop. There's a trimming two-foot swell out there with a space in the line-up just for me,' I tell him.

'I've got to go do a couple things before service tonight, Chef.' Jesse tries it on, like *now I'm worried*.

'Do not fuck with me tonight, Jesse. Do you understand me?'

'Yes, Chef,' Jesse answers.

'Seriously, though, we're close, you know what I mean?'

'Yes, Chef,' Jesse repeats.

And really, if I had any dignity left I wouldn't ask him where he's going or what he's doing but I don't and I ask him.

'What do you *have* to do in town, Jesse?'

And the boys stop what they're doing, just for a beat, and turn to catch my back soaping up the wall.

'Just got to see a man about a dog,' Jesse replies, like it's none of my fucking business.

And that's when I stop scrubbing and turn toward the boys.

'See a man about a dog . . . You know my dog is the biggest and angriest dog of them all, don't you, Jesse?'

'Yes, Chef!' Jesse laughs. 'I'll be back for service, Chef.'

'He's not a little puppy dog that you take for a walk and follow behind picking up his doggy-do-do. He's a big fierce dog who eats little kiddies and small cows.'

'Yes, Chef!' Jesse yells, and claps again. 'Service!'

'We're booked out again tonight, yeah? There's work to be done,' I remind him.

'Yes, Chef.' Jesse meets my eye. 'I won't be long, Chef. I've just got to go into town and then I'll be straight back to box my section.'

'Okay. Sounds like a plan. You coming for a surf, Soda?'

'Nah, Chef. I'll probably just head into town with Jesse.'

'Okay,' I say as I return to my cleaning. I'm nervous now. I know the boys are up to something.

And then, like a siren sounding, Sammy the barman gives the call we've all been waiting for.

'Vinnie's in the house!'

15

Bruce, my friend from the Bondi Hotel days, was working with me again at the Pasta Man. He was a few years older than me, and one of those guys who always seemed to be at the party. He was a right-place-right-time kind of guy. But he wasn't into narcotics; he was more a champagne and bong man. And when he suggested a road trip back up the highway to our home state of Queensland, he did so because he was worried about my drug use. I think he felt that if I could get back in touch with something innocent, like Queensland or home, I might be able to arrest my self-destructive ways and actually make something good out of the opportunity that the Pasta Man represented. And the idea of the tropics was appealing. I had written off my last misadventure into Kings Cross as a silly mistake, a youthful misadventure.

I had lost my licence on three separate occasions as a drunken young apprentice chef, so I left it to Bruce to hire the car. Which turned into a nightmare anyway because between us we didn't have a credit card with any credit left on it, which meant I had to stump up a cash deposit. Obviously the seven hundred dollars required to rent the car wasn't hanging around in petty cash at this point, so I did my friends in Brisbane a favour and offered to transport some smack up to the Sunshine State if they were prepared to pay upfront. Amazing really, the optimism of junkies. No worries, mate; sounds like a plan. And the thing is, my 'friends' had recently robbed a bank in the manner of some idiots from a two-dollar weekly they'd picked up at Video Ezy, and got busted. They were hungry for something to numb the pain of an impending prison sentence and, because they had been staying home with Mum, were able to come up with the money.

Getting busted on the freeway between Gosford and Sydney at two in the morning in the middle of winter for driving unlicensed and being fifty kilometres over the speed limit was not good. And what added heavily to that badness was the fact that I also had to dump the heroin out the window as we pulled the car over to talk to the police. This left me with some personal supply in the boot, which for a while there looked as if I was going to get busted for as well. The coppers, having established I'd made their night with on-the-spot fines, got to searching everything in the boot. I had seven deals in a film canister in my toiletry bag and it was the strangest sensation watching them as they poked through toothbrushes and aftershave, squeezed out toothpaste and tipped out pills . . . but never popped the lid off the little black film canister.

The thirty-kilometre ride back to Gosford in the police car was long and uncomfortable. And what made it worse was that, because the cops didn't find what they were looking for, they weren't interested in giving me a lift back up the highway to where they'd busted me. Bruce was a patient sort of guy and not one to act on instinct, meaning it would never occur to him to actually drive into Gosford and pick me up; rather he would sit there, in the middle of winter, wondering what the fuck he was doing on a drug-running trip to Queensland with someone who was clearly not on the up and up. Nor did the taxi driver have much sympathy. He insisted on getting paid before we left Gosford.

Brisbane didn't go well. The boys who'd paid for the smack were, to put it mildly, really looking forward to seeing me. When I explained to them that I'd been busted and had to dump their gear out the window, well, they understood it in a general sense but were nonetheless unimpressed. It was a hot and sticky few days, everyone hanging out and being quite nasty to each other. I'd put away the seven deals which were left in the film canister during the remainder of the car trip with Bruce, which meant I'd slept well in the car but now, in Brisbane, where winter doesn't visit with any real meaning, it was obvious a holiday in the tropics had not been a good idea.

I decided pretty quick that I never liked Brisbane anyway and in no time flat I was back wondering why I'd left my comfy rort in Newtown. Until I recalled that when I got back, it was time to start paying the Italians.

***

Johnnie could see the numbers crunching uncomfortably into something like hard work and on my first day back in Newtown we had a round-table meeting where he pretty much told me what he thought of both the business and me. Which was a load off for him. And then he gave me back his key to the shop, patted me on the head, and wished me all the best.

In three short months the business had come full circle. I was back doing seven days a week and was once more in dialogue with Doug and the Italians. In some ways that was good. It meant that I had to get my shit together and talk business. Of course they wanted to see the books, which was something I kept deferring, because the fantasyland I had created there was a Darklands—an inspired homily to the Jesus and Mary Chain album. And here's the thing about the Jesus and Mary Chain, my favourite band at the time: my friends in Brisbane, having got busted for the bank robbery and then disappointed by me, were still keen to do a deal. In fact they were sending someone down—a friend—who wanted to get on in a pretty big way and they were wondering if I could organise it. This was good; it was cream, which was something I was always keen to be covered in. And in what turned out to be good fortune, the Jesus and Mary Chain were playing around the corner at the Enmore Theatre on the night we agreed to do the deal—and I had tickets. What became apparent, though, was that the person the Brisbane boys had sent down to do the deal was a cop and he'd organised for about six of his undercover mates to have dinner at the Pasta Man on the night of the deal. Given how desperate I was for the cream, though, I thought I still might be able to outsmart the police and walk away with the folding.

I had known something wasn't right when the group of six booked a table. No one booked tables at the Pasta Man, it wasn't that kind of place. And the more they insisted on booking, the more suspicious I got. And when our 'friend' from Brisbane arrived and started showing off his gun, which was a police issue .38, I was just about convinced that in order to lessen their impending prison lag my mates from Brisbane had decided to cut a deal with the cops by throwing me to the lions. And I understood they were upset; they were down a couple of grand on the deal from a few weeks ago and they weren't the type of boys cut out to do time—but who is before you're the one that has to do it? The thing is, I really, really, really needed some money.

It took a fucking crowbar and then some to get the undercover cops out of the place before the mad, bad and evil Chris was prepared to do the deal. He wanted all the doors locked, the lights turned down and the punters outside. And given I had tickets to JMC, I used that as my excuse to get everyone out the door. Really, I don't know what they were thinking, six big burly blokes in Kmart suits and bad haircuts: they would have looked weird in here on any day of the week but tonight, alone in the cafe, en masse . . . well, it made me believe I might just get away with it.

Obviously when the detectives realised they were locked out of the deal they had to make a decision as to whether to send in the 'friend' from Brisbane. Thankfully they went ahead on what I can only imagine was an information-gathering mission. Their cash still went ker-ching so I didn't mind—and the concert, forget about it, those Scottish boys rocked.

A few weeks is a long time for a junkie down on his luck. And in the few weeks that followed my windfall from the federal police, I went to some places I don't really care to remember. Even during the worst of it, though, I was still obsessed with a couple of elements of hospitality. The first thing were my knives; their sharpness became paramount to me, the process of keeping them sharp a sort of stoned compulsion. The other obsession I had at that time was, not surprisingly, the fresh pasta. I became intrigued and then captivated by the various attributes of fresh pasta and the different techniques of cooking it. I was convinced that the al dente thing was actually an urban myth—some advertising campaign that had persuaded enough people that they knew something about pasta, where in fact what was happening was that a lot of people were getting indigestion from uncooked glutens.

I came to believe then, and have spoken to a lot of people since who should know about these things, that if you are going to make a dough and roll your pasta out with your wooden pin and work it between your fingers, you'll want to cook it off to al dente. And this means that in order to keep the fresh pasta alive and together, you don't want to overcook it, you want that tiny bit of texture when it comes time to eat it. If, on the other hand, you are using dried pasta or machine-made fresh pasta, you want to cook the shit out of it. And what I mean by that is if the pasta you're using can stand being boiled for a couple of minutes beyond al dente without falling apart, cook it to that degree and see if I'm wrong. It is important to capture some of the starch on the pasta. Do not rinse the cooked pasta. Simply scoop it out of the boiling water with tongs or a large steel spider (like a stainless-steel web), which allows the water to flood off the pasta as you transfer it to a bowl or pan. It's at this point that you oil and season the starchy pasta with salt and pepper, citrus zest, various herbs or whatever a particular dish calls for. Too many chefs try to get all the flavour into the sauce of a pasta dish rather than onto the pasta itself. Really, the sauce that accompanies pasta should be simple and tasty, not something that overpowers or dominates the beautifully seasoned linguine or fettuccine or tortellini.

Despite the sharpness of my knives and tastiness of pasta, my other problems wouldn't go away, and after some particularly harsh commentary in regards to my efforts at the accounting side of things, Doug and I decided to go our separate ways. I paid for the pasta a couple of times but what became apparent given the business model I had set in train—the one which saw me require a gram of smack a day in order to function—was that the investors in the business never were going to see a return on their capital.

When I handed in the keys I left unpaid bills and overdue rent. I left the place a mess and walked away. I had a heroin habit that was now so far inside me—into the very knots and fibre of my being—that I was a slave to it. There was nothing else that mattered to me other than where my next shot of smack was coming from, and I left the Pasta Man without a backward glance or thought for anyone else. And since I now had no money or income stream, I did what any loser down on his luck does: I phoned home.

in very [...] and [...] of my being. That I was a slave [...] There was nothing [...] that mattered to me other [...] the [...], the next [...] that was coming. I was [...] to [...] to Pasta Man without a backward glance or [...] thought of tomorrow. Yet I didn't know how bad things [...] to become as I still didn't know how low down on the [...] line I prepared to [...]

16

My mother had found another Prince Charming and been saved. She really didn't want me ruining the scene either. She was comfortably ensconced in Woollahra real estate, out by the pool on sunny days and off shopping on the expense account when the weather turned inclement. She was genuinely happy and truly believed that this was the real deal; her and hubby couldn't be happier and it was simply a matter of enjoying the ever-after bit.

While the mood was so positive I thought it best to act decisively and ticked the latest Charlie up for a seriously large motorbike and a place to stay up north. It wasn't an entirely cynical move; I was so far gone on the smack and so emotionally and physically fucked after the Pasta Man that I was determined to clean up my act. Charlie had a hundred-acre block of flat, barren land west of Too-woomba that was worth about a hundred dollars and he said I was welcome to pitch a tent out there in order to go through whatever I needed to go through. He even smiled when he suggested that no one would bother me.

Tara is a ghost town and I stayed a while. I got straight and my hair grew out into its natural colour for the first time in years. I was pleased to be clean; I wasn't drinking alcohol or smoking weed, only going into town every few weeks to pick up some fresh supplies. The block of land presented a harsh landscape. The trees were gnarly and mean and struggled to maintain the appearance of growth in a setting that was littered with decay. I pitched a tent in one of the few shady spots and my biggest challenge quickly became keeping the bush mice away so that the snakes didn't make my campsite their permanent home. I was on their level, sleeping on a blanket inside an Yves Klein blue two-man tent. I was a surface creature, an animal attached to the earth. All around me was dust and hot, pressing nature. And although culture had forged meaning into this landscape too, I felt part of something larger and stronger than the ephemera of culture's way. So much so that after a few months I began to feel semi-normal again and convinced myself that hell, as they say, was other people rather than a world of my own making.

I saved some of my government cheques, got the motorbike serviced and began to consider heading back into town. And town this time would be Brisbane. There was no way I going back to Sydney: too many bad memories, too many blazing bridges. Brisbane . . . Even the sound of the name put me to sleep. It sounded safe and warm, a cosy place where a burnt-out kid might start again. And besides, I knew some good people there.

My first trip back into town was more fraught than I'd imagined it would be. Considering that I'd left Sydney in a blaze of pain, I wasn't concerned about things like having a licence to ride the Honda 750 I was on; I wasn't worried about the out-of-date registration label or the outstanding warrants I had from my Gosford trip gone wrong. I had underestimated what being back in a city meant. Every police car and red light, every bottle shop and happy family, crowded in on me to the point where I got shaky, vulnerable, and I didn't like it.

My first joint sliced the edge off things nicely. I hooked back up with Angela and caught up with some old friends. I took to hanging out in the local hotel and shooting pool and staying calm. The idea of not using any drugs at all hadn't occurred to me. I was convinced that my problem was heroin and as long as I stayed away from injecting that, everything else would work out fine. My levels of anxiety convinced me that I couldn't stay in town permanently, however, and I spent the next few months riding back and forth between the block of land and Brisbane. And I didn't get lonely for months. It was strange how far a sense of shame or disappointment will keep a person from wanting contact with others. I knew I had blown a great opportunity at the Pasta Man; blown it badly. After a few tastes of Brisbane, though, I was starting to feel the need for company and other people more often. I began to think that what I was looking for out on the property, being alone with nature, was in fact an illusion. It started to feel like what I was doing was running away and what I really needed to do was back myself in the city by getting another job in a kitchen somewhere and making a proper go of things.

17

Sammy has a neat row of coffee cups and petits fours lined up along the bar for Paris and the girls. And as Vinnie bounds up the stairs with his girlfriend Jackie, he looks a little bedraggled, a little like he's been interrupted from a particularly sweet dream in order to attend an emergency.

Scotty guides Jackie to a table as Vinnie makes a beeline for the kitchen.

'You guys know what you're doing?' Vinnie asks from his command position in the bar.

'Yes, Chef,' I reply in a fashion that indicates I don't want to piss him off any more than he obviously is. Now is not the time to be a smart-arse with Vinnie: that's just what he's looking for, someone to unload on for being a wise guy when he should have known better.

'What the fuck is Paris Hilton doing in my restaurant?' he asks, shaking his head and lighting a cigarette.

'No one books any more, Vinnie. It's a disgrace,' I say.

'Fucking kitchen's a mess, mate. What are you blokes doing?'

'We're onto it, Vinnie. We're going to scrub down now and get ready for dinner. We're booked out again tonight,' I tell him.

'Of course we're fucking booked out, Jimmy. It's New Year's Day, you clown. It's the only time we ever make any money. It's costing me a fortune just to keep the doors of this place open.' Vinnie launches into what's become a familiar refrain.

'Scotty,' Vinnie calls out to the maître d', who has just returned from seating Jackie and delivering the coffees to Paris's table. 'Don't bother ringing me when my friends turn up, mate. I don't own the fucking place or anything.'

Scotty has been rehearsing his next lines for a couple of hours now. And Vinnie is aware of that and is keen to disrupt Scotty's thought patterns in order to gain an early advantage so that he can justify laying the blame where everyone knows it's going to end up anyway.

'Don't tell me my phone was off either, you could've called Jackie or GT or anyone else to let me know I had friends dropping in for lunch. I hope you've looked after everyone, mate. If I go out there and hear anything other than that I'm a genius and they want to move into my hotel permanently, I'll fucking sack you, all right?'

'Yes, Vinnie,' Scotty replies, not stopping long enough to listen to anything else the boss has to say. And really, Scotty has heard it all before, but that doesn't lessen an onlooker's joy in watching the kill.

'I might just sack you anyway,' Vinnie calls after him.

Then he turns abruptly. 'Don't you fucking laugh, Jesse. What were the police doing in my hotel this morning? Yeah, I heard all about it, mate. You think I don't know everything that goes on in my hotel? And you—if I catch you smoking weed one more time you're gone, all right?' Vinnie tells Choc. And he's serious: seriously pissed off and completely sober. Which is rare and a little more real than anyone is used to.

And it's not that Vinnie isn't a good bloke when he's not drinking, it's just that he's been caught off guard by Paris and her crew coming for lunch and not phoning ahead. He's unsure how to play this one out. Part of him is angry that the dickhead who brought her here didn't let him know they were coming, and another part of him is wanting to be the gracious host anyway and lay on a few drinks and treat them all like the rock stars they want to be. But the fact they didn't call him . . . you can feel it winning the battle between good host/hurt friend.

'Are you and Jackie joining Paris for lunch, Vinnie?' I ask him, trying to break the tension.

'Fuck them, mate. They've already eaten. Give me a small steak and chips with mustard—and I mean small, all right? Don't send me out half a cow again or I'll sack you too.'

'Yes, Chef,' I reply. 'Jackie having the fish?'

'Yeah, give her the fucking fish,' Vinnie sighs. 'And not too big, she's getting fat.'

'Yes, Chef,' I say, nodding, careful not to laugh. There's a time to joke with Vinnie and a time to do what you're told and say as little as possible. Some people don't understand that and they tend not to stay long at Rae's. Vinnie doesn't want the truth, or anything that smells remotely like it: he wants what he wants and if you can't figure out what that is—well then, you're a silly cunt who doesn't know anything.

'Fucking Scotty,' Vinnie says, shaking his head as he stubs out his cigarette and walks off into the restaurant to take a seat at his table with Jackie.

The thing about Rae's on Watego's is that it's not like a lot of other fine-dining restaurants or large hotels. It's a really small and intimate space that Vinnie owns and runs like his personal mansion for a select group of friends. If you stay at Rae's, you're a friend of Vinnie's. And if you're not rich and famous before you arrive, you're going to feel that way from the moment you pull into the drive.

'You still going into town, Jesse?' I ask.

'I've got to, Chef. I won't be long,' Jesse answers. And now I know that whatever's going on for the boys is fairly serious. Jesse wouldn't risk a shouting match with Vinnie if the stakes weren't high.

'It's no biggie, Chef. I've just got to see someone about a room in their house.'

'Are you moving?' I ask.

'Yeah, I've got to,' Jesse replies.

'Get Vinnie's salad started, okay?' I tell him.

'Yes, Chef.'

'Not a good time to be moving, Jesse.' I state the obvious, again.

And Jesse and Soda laugh dismissively, like, *no kidding, Einstein.*

'Soda, get back on the dishes, mate. Jesse can finish up his section now.'

'Yes, Chef,' says Soda, who takes it like a man and heads back down to the steaming end of things.

'Let me know if you get stuck, Jesse, all right?' I insist.

At which Jesse turns around and nods. 'Thanks, Chef.'

'I mean it. I know you don't really want to move in with Alice and the boys, but there are alternatives to having nowhere to live.'

'Yes, Chef,' Jesse replies. And I know he wants me to just shut up and let him handle this. And I would—normally—but physically, I cannot do both his section and mine. If I have to do both sections because he loses the plot over moving house or anything else, it will break me. That's what I know. And I might not know very much else about anything much, but I know that having to do Jesse's section as well as mine will send me into a space where I might shatter into very tiny pieces. And no one wants that. This is a party house in a party town. All anyone wants is to have a good time; blow off some cobwebs and a few of last year's disappointments and loves gone wrong. It's not a crime to want to suck back some pleasure at this time of year. The hell of Christmas with family and weirdo relatives has been and gone; all the broken dreams of last year have magically disappeared via the countdown last night and now . . . it's a new dawn. And on this brand-new day, this fresh and forgiving New Year's Day, people are entitled not to be stuffed around by some dickheads in the kitchen who couldn't organise a picnic basket. Really, I understand that. I had the high season off once too. It's just that there are limits to what a man can do. And given that Jesse has let the line down before by not turning up, I feel compelled to ensure it doesn't happen again.

Last time Jesse didn't turn up for work it was understandable: his girlfriend had got drunk and taken up with someone else while they were all out at a nightclub. I could feel his pain, but it was me that had to pick up the pieces and do his section as well as mine. I got away with it then because it was winter. Rae's is not busy in winter; some days we do no one at all in the restaurant. You spend all day prepping up your section's *mise en place* and then, during service, kill an hour or two staring out to sea with Scotty in the restaurant. We still have to bake the bread rolls for lunch; we still have to pound the *nahm jim* in the mortar and pestle for the freshly shucked oysters At the end of service, we either have a staff lunch or throw the lot out and prepare everything again for dinner. The small quantities we prepare reflect the reality of not having any bookings—and, of course, we are obliged to keep the food costs to a minimum. The cold months in Byron Bay can be a wasteland in the hospitality industry.

But that's not the quality of problem we have today. From Christmas Day through till the end of January we are booked out. Every room, every lunch and dinner service, the place is bursting with people looking to have the time of their lives. It's a blast—for them. Generally speaking, everyone knows what they're in for at Rae's because they've been before, and most of them will stick their heads into the kitchen and say 'Hi' or 'Thanks' or, if they're on a first-name basis with the chefs, 'You're a disgrace, Jimmy. That was terrible,' and then run off, giggling, to the bathrooms. It's a real gas.

'Why do you have to move now, Jesse?' I ask, frustrated. And I know I shouldn't say anything, I know everything will probably work out fine, but I can't let it go.

'Fuck, Chef!' Jesse shouts, and storms out of the kitchen. 'I'm going for a cigarette.'

'Two minutes!' I call after him. And that's being generous. You can't have your line cooks telling you how things are going to go. That just doesn't work. It never worked that way when I was down the line and it's not going to work like that at Rae's—not today or any time soon.

'He could stay at my girlfriend's place, Chef, if he gets stuck,' Choc suggests in his good-natured way. And when he says it, I can see Soda down at the dirty end of things smile and shake his head like, *which boat did you just get off?*

'That's very nice of you, Choc. Too bloody nice, mate. But I wouldn't let Jesse anywhere near your girlfriend when you're not around.'

And Choc laughs. He's a Kiwi, he's young and generous, and where he comes from everyone's family.

'He wouldn't want to drive out to Dunoon anyway, I guess.'

'No, mate, he probably wouldn't,' I say.

What Choc doesn't quite get is that, while it's imperative Jesse turns up to work and takes his place on the line, he's nothing more than a bundle of frazzled nerves and overtired muscles. Working long hours in such a small, hot, cramped space, surrounded by other men, has made him desperate for anything that might remotely function as a form of relief. And you don't leave people like that unattended around your loved ones. It's not fair. What you do is keep them on a very short leash and you tug it every now and then in order to keep their mind on the job.

I open the oven and squeeze Vinnie's steak between my forefinger and thumb to check where it's at: another three minutes. I season Jackie's piece of fish and press it into a very hot pan, skin side down. It's a small piece of fish, just like Vinnie asked for. It's smaller than Jackie will want but its size will give Vinnie some perverse satisfaction, particularly if she complains, which will open the door for Vinnie to start nagging her about her weight. That Jackie is slender, fit and trim is not the point. The point is, Vinnie is pissed off, aggravated and skinny and he prefers everyone around him to be pissed off, aggravated and skinny.

Out through the pass I can see that Vinnie has positioned his chair so that his back is towards Paris and her friends. This sets him apart from the other diners in the restaurant, all of whom have their chairs casually aligned so that they are able to both eat their meals and converse with their lunch companions while simultaneously staring at Paris Hilton. I don't know what it is about some famous people that manage to pull focus in such a magnetic way. Most people will cop a look at someone famous if they're in the same vicinity, but Paris seems to have become something more than that; she's a weird cultural fascinator constantly caught in the light of other people's gaze.

When media commentators talk about Paris Hilton as if she's some sort of strange, nothing celebrity, famous for being famous, I would argue they miss the point. Last time I checked she's famous for being a brain-bogglingly rich heir to a hotel fortune. And she's been in the spotlight for that reason (as well as the fact she's okay to look at) since anyone can remember. And cooking lunch for her while she's in a hotel restaurant seems somehow right. I've got no doubt she never stays at any Hilton hotel, or if she does it's in a room I don't know about, because she's far too classy for that brand. She's a fucking ambassador for God's sake, for her and her family's fortune. Having Paris constantly in the media, commented on and commenting on various topics, is like having a blank cheque to market your hotel chain. No one else might have noticed, but I seem to recall that the Hilton hotel chain has refurbished just about every high-rise building they own in the last few years. They have probably done that because they can afford to, and the reason they can afford to is quite possibly because Paris has made what was fast becoming a crusty seventies brand sexy all over again.

Part of Paris's image problem is no doubt tied up with perceptions of what constitutes hospitality. For some—and their numbers thin out as you get into the five-star end of things—hospitality is simply a service industry that caters to the most functional aspects of travelling: a bed to sleep in and a room to call one's own for a night, while the serious business happens during the daylight hours, away from the hotel itself. The hospitality industry is a sort of necessary evil for those travellers in the sense that you have to take your body with you. But that's not how it is for people with either substantial amounts of money or a keen appreciation for the finer things in life. For this select group of individuals, hospitality makes up their most treasured memories and they love nothing more than to capture an audience with stories about their favourite chalet in Norway or their top-secret guest-house on the south-west tip of France where Alain, the owner/chef, prepares the most exquisite little pastries for morning tea. And the wine at Chablis! Really, for those people, hospitality is like the meaning of life; it's what gets them out of their king-size beds each morning. And the secret of their passion lies in how they have inverted the rubric of hospitality whereby the discovery, appreciation and conversation about the various and complex ways in which hospitality might be delivered and enjoyed becomes the reason to travel, rather than a necessary extravagance of any particular journey.

Given that everyone needs to eat at least a couple of times a day and to sleep at some point, the how, what, when and where of those universal needs describes what hospitality does. For some people, meeting those needs is an art form. It's what they most like doing. As a chef, I don't often get to know what these people do or how they come by their money, but since everyone has a choice about how they spend their own dollars and cents, the people for whom hospitality is not so much a luxury as a goal are my kind of people. They are not so much critics as connoisseurs, carefully weighing up various elements of a particular dish or glass of wine or the quality of a hotel's sheets. And they are not just looking for what is familiar; if that was their goal they'd return to what pleases them most and never stay in new places. But that's not what they want; they are looking for new and ever different ways to experience hospitality. And given that notions of what constitutes the new will never end, the search for the next extraordinary hospitality experience becomes the reason for the journey.

The perception that the hospitality industry is a sort of large, indestructible, slow-to-change business model that functions the same way across the globe is deeply flawed. The reality is that most restaurants don't last more than a couple of years and that if hotels don't constantly reinvent themselves, they go out of business. What never changes about the hospitality industry is the need for hospitality; what functions as an aspect of that industry is constantly evolving. Just as chefs job-hop from one restaurant to the next, so do hotels open and close. Empty spaces that are set up to provide hospitality are constantly bought and sold, their stainless-steel skeletons inspiring an endless chain of spaces that, when they are brought back to life, describe what the hospitality industry is at any given time.

'Vinnie wants a bowl of chips with his steak,' Scotty barks into the kitchen.

'Everyone friends out there?' I ask.

'Paris and the girls are leaving,' Scotty says.

'They going now?' Jesse asks as he barges his way back into the kitchen after sucking back a cigarette.

'Yeah,' says Scotty as he dumps empty coffee cups and petits fours plates smudged with melted chocolate onto the waiter's station.

18

It took me a while to get settled in Brisbane after having spent six months in a two-man tent in the middle of nowhere. Angela and I had decided to keep things reasonably casual—at least Angela had—and I eventually moved into an unoccupied corner at Bruce's place. He'd moved on with his life and wasn't bearing any grudges over the Gosford calamity. My greatest asset was that I was physically healthy again after so much time in the bush. And although I was a little fragile without the drugs, I was still able to function and was keen to make every step a winner.

I applied for a position as a chef de partie at the Barracks in Paddington and got the job. The section I would be running was pasta, which was fine by me. After the Pasta Man, I was keen to be thought of as an expert in anything that didn't involve shooting up drugs. The kitchen at the Barracks was relatively new and well equipped. This was something I was unfamiliar with. The kitchens I had worked in to date had been put together in histories previous to my time on Planet Earth and had been adapted to suit their most recent incarnations. This is not an unusual phenomenon; many commercial kitchens have at least one major cooking appliance that is surplus to its current needs given that it was machinery required for a previous menu. Such implements will often trigger a new menu, dreamt up by a new chef eager to employ the unused technology. The Barracks, though, had just undergone a major reconstruction and its new owners had spent good money on the kitchen, which was designed around the idea of churning out vast quantities of pasta with ragu-style sauces that were displayed and served from a heated stone bain-marie.

The line-up at the Barracks was a three-chef affair. Head chef Kevin did the pans, Graham did sauce and fryers, and I did the pasta. It wasn't fine dining but it did have its strengths, the first of which was that we were very busy.

What makes one restaurant busy and another one, often right next door to the busy one, a fire pit for money is not as simple an equation as some people might think. Of course when it's pumping and the staff are busy and customers are having a great time and the owners are making plenty of money and everyone's happy it's easy to say what makes a restaurant successful: it's everything we're doing, stupid. But the actual formula is more complex. If, for instance, you take the same concept and move it to another suburb, the new rendition of the successful formula can often die a spectacular death. Sometimes those places are empty from opening night and don't improve. The owners will spend good money from the successful enterprise to prop up the failed one, sure that in time people will catch on.

'It's the same as this one over here that everyone loves so much and as soon as you all find out where we are, it's going to go off.'

But it doesn't. So the owners close up shop, write off the few hundred thousand it cost to start up, and return to concentrate on the mystery of why this particular place is as successful as it is. And often a reasonably small thing can tip a place over from being successful to being an empty cave with candles: a new chef, a new maître d', new decor, new menu, a bad write-up in the papers, or indeed the inverse of all those things: they needed a chef, the menu was tired, they put the prices up because they got a good review. And again, some places are just always successful, the institutions that ride out recessions, bad reviews, incompetent chefs and rude waiters. Everywhere has limits to such antics but the institutions, those truly rare beasts that thrive over decades, generally have a few things in common.

The most common trait of the institutional restaurant is one particular personality. They might own the real estate or be the chef or run the floor or just hang about the place, but the single most common thread among such successful places is one person. It's what people think of when they think of the restaurant, and often the restaurant will be named after that person or at least will become known as a direct expression of that person's efforts at hospitality. And whether it's Lucio's, Rae's, Sergio's, Musso and Frank's or Betty's Bistro, a person who has talent and sticks—which is no certainty in hospitality—will often survive and even prosper in times of cultural change and upheaval, the sheer familiarity of the place providing a light in a storm.

The other primary reason that some restaurants become institutions is because of their location. Everyone wants to eat at some point on his or her trip to the Grand Canyon, and if you own the leasehold or freehold of a joint that hangs over the lip of such a location, you're probably going to do all right. These restaurants are known as view restaurants. It might be ocean, mountain, wilderness, canyon, waterfall, zoo, cityscape or Times Square; the restaurant might also revolve, have picture-frame windows, outdoor seating or a combination of all three. The most important thing about these institutional restaurants, though, is that they are invariably a worse dining experience than the institutional places which are named after the people that own them.

The Barracks belonged to that other great restaurant tradition, the themed restaurant. The Barracks of the restaurant's title referred to the fact that the dungeon, which constituted the restaurant space, was previously a prison barracks. That a hotel had been built on top of where a prison barracks once stood meant that now the place was a fortitude of pleasure rather than a dungeon of despair—at least most of the time.

The pasta at the Barracks was dried linguine and came in three flavours: spinach, tomato and egg. It got cooked to al dente in a large pot of salted boiling water and then tipped out onto a stainless-steel bench with holes in it that allowed the water to flood through. Importantly, the pasta wasn't washed, which meant it remained coated in starch.

While the pasta was still hot it would be transferred to a large stainless-steel bowl and doused in olive oil. Olive oil here is fat and its very liberal use is critical. And because olive oil is cheap (though revered) in Italy, no one thinks about the price of the oil when they are using it. And I find that is a good approach to any food I'm preparing: think about taste and pleasure first and costs when you have to. So the pasta was oily and, despite all the starch, moved freely about the stainless-steel bowl. Next I would wind a pile of linguine around the fingers of my left hand. Initially I would use a set of scales to determine that each 'bunch' of linguine constituted a serve, which I would place on a flat tray, each serve with a hole in the centre where my fingers had been. Pretty soon I didn't need the scales, the single-serve portions becoming so obvious that I could determine any string of pasta plus or minus in an instant.

The serve-size bundles of pasta set quite hard as they cooled, each tray going into the coolroom until service, whereupon they would be brought out and placed above my pasta sink. A pasta sink is a large, square, stainless-steel tub with baskets—much like a deep fryer—but filled with water rather than oil. And the water would be kept at just below boiling point, which meant things got steamed up in my section. As a service progressed, the water evaporated, and I had to turn on the tap above the sink in order to keep the heating elements covered. Over the course of a three- or four-hour service the water would become so starchy from so many pasta bundles being plunged into it that it would develop a skin that would have to be scooped out with a spider and tossed. But the starch was good; it was flavour.

After the pasta was plunged into the hot water and left for a minute it would swell and go just over al dente, which is where you want it, before turning it out into a small stainless-steel bowl. Then salt flakes, pepper, fresh oregano, orange zest, nutmeg or lemon juice would be added from the rows of *mise en place*. Each pasta dish had its own combination of flavours and a different stainless-steel bowl. And as the service went on and the pasta water got thicker with starch and the stainless-steel bowls became truly seasoned and the resting pasta sweated yeast and gluten, the flavours became more pronounced, more intense. And although things could tip over and go too far—blowing over into a yeasty nightmare—everyone agreed that the best pastas came out at the end of the night. It was a process that couldn't be replicated by adding more flavours earlier in the night; it was more the combination of time, heat, fats and chemical reactions that over the course of a service built flavours into the process.

Since arriving back in Brisbane I had managed to avoid my friends who used heroin. It wasn't hard; they didn't dine out where I worked, and I worked all the time. Then one night Duane stumbled into the Barracks. Seeing him again after a couple of years made it obvious we'd both changed since our poorly organised drug run between

Sydney and Brisbane. And despite his insistence he'd let all that go, I wasn't entirely convinced he'd forgiven me for arriving in town—after my detour to Gosford—with no drugs and none of his money.

'Nah, nah, I've moved on, Jimmy,' he kept saying when I asked him about it. 'Really, mate, it was a couple of years ago. Shit happens,' he said.

And while he was correct about that, I couldn't shake the feeling that I owed him something.

Things went really well for the first couple of hours. We sucked back a couple of beers and caught up on two years' worth of general gossip, and then, just as things were winding down, he said he had to go meet someone. Did I want to come along? And when he said that, he glanced at me, almost imperceptibly. It was the same look that the hookers in Kings Cross used when I was looking to score.

No one works the streets if they're not a junkie. And the streets are where all junkies end up. The street worker's drug of choice might be coke but it's probably smack or a combination of both—and the look from Duane on that particular evening said the same thing—it said, *do you want to get on?* And my uncensored and ill-conceived response was 'Why not?'

And there were plenty of really good reasons why not but none of them flashed through my mind at the time. We finished our drinks and two minutes later were burning rubber on our way out of the hotel car park.

It wasn't long before I was back in the drug scene of Brisbane. And I'm not sure if things have got any better for drug-injecting users up there but, back in the day, the dope was shithouse and the service far from reliable. Which was frustrating. It often meant that if I wanted to score before work I would be more than forgivably late. I wasn't in a position to lose my job—this wasn't the routine that saw me turn up late a few days in a row in order to get the holiday pay; this was the routine controlling me. Which is never cool. I didn't want to acknowledge it at the time but chasing another rabbit down another hole in Brisbane meant that I was crossing another line. And this was a line that I was desperate not to fall over, because on the other side of the chalk was a suburb called Junkie.

When the hotel that housed the Barracks sold and the new owners wanted to make some changes, I wasn't ready for what they had in mind. It appeared Kevin was on some very large folding and the new owners decided they no longer needed him, at least not on that money. It meant that when Kevin and his sous-chef Graham walked out, I was the new head chef. Fuck, don't get me wrong, I was keen, hyped up and ready to flow—in spirit. It's just that my body required some pretty regular medical assistance—again—that I could only half please from the pharmacy. I was perhaps too quickly convinced that I had all the necessary skill and talent to be able to pull off the whole head chef thing of what was a pretty successful, though still quite new, restaurant.

Ads went in the paper for a new team and I hit the ground smoking. It was fun, for a while. I'd always had the capacity to do the hours, no problem. Angela and I were going along sweetly and, just to cap off the promotion, I decided to go rock-and-roll with the blue-black hair dye again. I was back on some decent money and really, things could only get worse.

I didn't change the menu very much. It wasn't like I was some Italian kid waiting for an opportunity to reveal his region's cuisine to the world; I was from the beef capital of Australia and had been trained in basic French cooking. I had become familiar with large prime cuts at the Bondi Hotel and fresh pasta at the Pasta Man. So what I did was palm off pasta to one of the new chefs, and moved down the line to stand at the head of things on the stove. And really, to this day, I'm most comfortable in front of a six-burner stove. I can struggle through larder or fry and even do pastry if you put a gun to my head, but the stove, with its cast-iron pans and docket spike, that's me. I figure it's because I like being in control when service hits. And I like it because I don't like being yelled at. Like I said, most chefs when they're under the pump turn into screamers, and the previous crew at the Barracks were no exception.

And it isn't that I don't communicate; no one can stand at the pass and call it while they cook grill section or pans and not communicate. At the most hectic times, the ability to do the job can be reduced to an ability to handle pressure; either you have it or you don't. And a bright reader who has been around too many back streets might put it all down to the drugs but, seriously, the worst, most aggro, most regretful services I've called have been when I was out of it on smack or crack or piss or

126

pills or the dreaded combination soup. Being in that state of things does not lend itself to being under pressure.

What became a normal day for me as head chef at the Barracks was to get in early and do all my prep and *mise en place* while I was comfortably stoned. Then, prior to service, I would have a cold shower or a swim or a micro-sleep or do whatever else I could to snap out of my drug-induced state, because service is show time, baby, and you need everything you've got.

The problems got more intense at the Barracks as the new owners became increasingly obsessed with cost cutting. I don't know how many geniuses I've met along the way in hospitality who think that by saving a few bucks here and a few bucks there, by pulling some from over this and under that, that the business starts to edge down. And when it starts to edge down they become more obsessed with paperwork and costs and chefs' hours and they lose sight of why they bought into hospitality in the first place. Everyone has to be creative about food and labour costs, but when the whole focus becomes the representation of the business rather than the business itself, particularly if it's hospitality, it falls to shit. Paperwork in restaurants is overrated. And I can hear all the college-trained executive hotel chefs spitting out their warm tea but really, paperwork is for the pixies; it's got nothing to do with cooking and I don't like to see people dressed up in chef's clobber sitting behind a desk in front of a mountain of paperwork. I figure that as head chef, if you can't do all the shop's paperwork in fifteen minutes at the end of the day you may as well call yourself a manager or an accountant or something else less kind. Hospitality is about pleasure and the human body, about the universal need to eat, drink and sleep. It's not about facts and figures and numbers and costs. Put the energy into a new menu, cleaning the chairs and baking the bread, and leave the paperwork to the pinheads.

Tuesday was the busiest night at the Barracks until the new owners killed it. They thought we weren't making enough margin on the night so they pulled the special, which was basically a two-for-one deal on the pasta. And maybe we weren't making a fortune on Tuesdays, but we were making something and, most importantly, we were turning over vast quantities of everything just after the weekend. And weekends are where every joint makes its money—other than the business lunch model—and you don't have to be Marco Pierre White to open on Friday and Saturday nights and do a few covers. But given that we knew we had Tuesday night to clear out the *mise en place*, we could prep the shit out of everything before the weekend, confident that should we not have a massive Friday and Saturday, we could clear it out on Tuesday.

Of course once the Tuesday night thing was dead they jacked the prices up for the rest of the week. It was like watching Thomas the Tank Engine leave the rails. Every decision the new owners took obviously made sense in the office, but they failed to treat the punters who came and ate and drank and paid our bills as people with the capacity to make decisions. It was as if all the projections they made were somehow the truth of things and people were simply going to conform to their business plans. But that didn't happen and pretty soon things were too quiet for a line of three chefs and then too quiet for a line of two and not long after that it was me and Stanus the kitchen hand. And she was a good old girl, more kitchen porter than kitchen hand, which meant she could function as a very reliable prep chef. The problem was that the new owners had pretty much squeezed the fun out of the joint and the more that happened the more the punters stopped coming and the more time I had to indulge in my less productive habits. And it was just as well I had the time because it took far too much of that resource to get anything like stoned in Brisbane. Every time I got ripped off or skimmed or sold ninety percent glucose that some of the locals thought was the dope . . . I could hear Sydney calling.

Although there's a lot of years between me at the Barracks then and me at Rae's on Watego's today, before I left the Barracks I ate at a joint called Faces which was doing good business. It was here that I met a much younger Vinnie Rae. This was his first restaurant and had all the hallmarks of what would become his recipe for success. First of all the place was pumping; it was sexy, expensive and covered in glory. People who worked for him were doing a hundred hours a week and getting paid for forty; the food looked great on what were expensive plates and for me, it was an introduction to fine dining. And everything made sense except the wages. I just couldn't figure out how I'd cope going back to what was an apprentice chef wage after tasting the pay cheques of a head chef. I had hundreds of dollars a week spare as a head chef to do what I wanted with. While I chose to believe that I didn't have to use the quantities of drugs I had been for the last few years, really, the choice about those things had already been made. I wasn't about to sacrifice five hundred a week to learn how to make a better-quality jus. No, it was the nightlife for me, baby: I was cursed with that neon gene.

19

Leaving the Barracks and Brisbane wasn't a difficult choice in the end. There was a night there, right at the end of things, when after hanging around the hotel and getting completely smashed, I projectile vomited into a group of friends without bothering to get out of my chair. Which is difficult PR for anyone to spin. It was a vomit that took me, as well as my friends, by surprise. Smack makes everyone vomit, it's just par for the course, but lately I'd been getting very tired of having to run off to the toilets and dry-retch so I had fallen into the habit of simply bending down or turning away from people and sort of heaving into my sleeve before turning back to the table of friends or pretty girls with *what the fuck are you looking at? eyes.* How bad could it be? If I hadn't eaten for a while or had been dry-retching for a few hours prior, I figured it was a pretty safe bet that nothing was going to come up this time and I could save myself the inconvenience of having to walk to the bathrooms. How I got it so very wrong on that particular night is still a mystery to me. Even more unfortunate was that, in my attempts to try out new things, I figured that if I didn't actually turn away from people any more, the heaving action would be less noticeable. As a technique, I still don't write it off completely, but I can also categorically state that there is no sure way of knowing whether you're going to have a dry run or actually spew up about four litres of Italian *mise en place*.

People were growing tired of me in Brisbane and that was something I was both embarrassed about and unfamiliar with. I was used to being quite popular and, generally speaking, close to the centre of things. During the last few months, though, people had started to treat me with disdain. I was in my mid-twenties and that fact alone seemed to forgive a lot of illicit behaviour, but there was also little doubt that my drug intake was being perceived by others as something that was running the show rather being on the periphery of things, like it was for them. And, sadly, all the time I had spent out west on the block of land getting straight, getting to know myself and get the fuck over Newtown had disappeared from my short-term memory. It was like it had never happened and my heroin habit had picked up from where I'd left it in Sydney. And it was pissed off with me for leaving it behind. It had grown lonely and weird during my absence and now it was demanding an ever-larger speaking part. Such demands were expensive and diffi-cult to please given the quality of the local dope.

I found myself up to old tricks with the cash register and late with the rent. I found myself selling the car I'd managed to buy and watching in mild disbelief as I hocked my guitar. Again. And I also found that despite the extra money I was earning as head chef, it was, as the song goes, never enough. Like a lot of other losers I'd met, I heard myself constantly talking about how the problem was the supply side of things, how if I could just get the supply-and-demand cycle right, everything else would be peaches and cream. The more I listened to myself acting like that and talking like that, the easier it was to accept the logic that once a junkie always a junkie. And it wasn't like it was something in the drug, some incomprehensible element of heroin that meant I was unable to stop using for any length of time; it was more that I told myself I simply preferred being a junkie. I was no longer able to locate the necessary motivation to actively want to be anything else. The irony was that being a junkie required a great deal of commitment; it required energy, enthusiasm, ambition and an enormous amount of self-will. It was like each day I awoke with a vital mission. And while there were plenty of days I didn't want to go on that mission, days I wanted the mission to self-destruct, it never did: it just got harder and harder, the scams more daring and dangerous, the potential for everything to go wrong closer to the surface.

On the morning after my unfortunate vomit, I sensed that it would be in my best interests to put some distance between myself and the people I called friends, a little breathing space that smelt of clean air and fresh opportunity rather than public bar carpet. Obviously I still had my perceptive faculties about me and, after collecting a few weeks' holiday pay and sending flowers to various ports, I bought a bus ticket to Sydney.

It wasn't hard at the time to write the whole place off and the people too as I boarded a bus out of Brisbane. Sydney! Yeah, baby, I was coming back and this time, well, I'd straighten up first and get some cash together but then I was going straight to the top. I figured I could be covered in glory with about six months of genuine effort and hard work. I even started to lower my tolerance before I left and had begun exercising. I was confident I had sufficient skills now as a chef to fit into any number of kitchen situations. The hardest choice I had in regards to work was whether to join a large brigade in a fine-dining joint as a chef de partie—maybe grill section or larder—or work as a head chef in a small place where the glory was negligible but the money was great.

I bought all the Sydney newspapers before I left town and scoured the positions vacant. There were many opportunities for an ambitious young chef. And I probably would have done very well in any number of the advertised positions if I had followed that plan.

After a particularly taxing journey on the overnight bus, I figured I might rip up to Kings Cross and get a seven am pick-me-up before heading over to Balmain, where I had organised to crash with my brother and his young family. Seven am is what's known colloquially around Kings Cross as Desperate Hour, when the lowest of the low and the ugliest of the ugly vie with each other to be the very lowest and/or ugliest. It's actually good sport if you manage to get comfortably stoned and a ringside seat at one of the early openers. Failing that—which is to say if you're out among it trying to score or cut a deal—well, you're fair game, my son.

While a part of me still felt ashamed about my vomiting session at the Barracks in far-off Brisbane, here in Kings Cross I was a veritable cleanskin. Until I got ripped off and found myself more in the thick of things, and much sooner too, than I might have imagined. What began with the reasonably simple idea that I deserved a little self-medicated relief after a too-long night on a too-crowded bus quickly turned into a welcome home that made my Brisbane sojourn look like a time of moral fortitude and prudent restraint. In fact, what became apparent by about quarter past eight was that it was only the unavailability of what might reasonably be called heroin that meant I was able to hold things together for as long as I had in Brisbane.

At lunchtime I knocked on the door of my brother's house. He had kindly agreed to let me crash in his garage until I got myself sorted, and getting sorted was something I was overly optimistic about now that I was partially stoned. Like a lot of junkies, I had fallen into that cliché of optimism about what I was going to do—tomorrow. It was a circle of desiring various things from life, then being sated with drugs rather than the original things that I desired. And it was a narrative that seemed to provide the script for my addictive ways: each shot both ending the desperate nature of my desire and diminishing the chance of ever being able to realise anything other than using more drugs.

20

As Paris and her entourage get up from the table to leave Rae's, there's a general scattering of waiters, scraping of chairs and turning of heads from staff and other lunch guests. The colour and movement of Paris leaving the building seems to deserve one last stare from the punters who did, after all, share lunch with the girls.

Vinnie remains stubbornly turned away from the fracas. One of the security guys returns to take up his position near the kitchen doorway and the other security guy crosses his arms at the entrance to the restaurant. The handsome young bookmaker who is a star of the social pages and who organised the outing with Paris today pays Scotty for lunch with a crisp pile of hundred-dollar bills.

'How was the fish?' I ask Mr Security.

'Excellent, Chef,' he replies and gives me two thumbs up. 'Busy in here today.'

'It's New Year's Day, you clown, of course we're fucking busy,' says Jesse, his voice dripping with contempt.

'Fucking Jesse . . .' I say, shaking my head.

'Really?' The security guy plays along with Jesse, looking at his watch like Dumbo the Clown.

But Jesse's response is exactly why this guy is standing at the kitchen doorway rather than at the restaurant entrance with the other security guy. He's seen it all before, and while it is a little disconcerting to have a very large man basically obstruct my kitchen staff from going about their business—should they need to leave the kitchen—I figure he's been found out before by more than one smart-arse young chef.

'Glad you enjoyed your lunch,' I tell him.

'Yeah, it was the best feed I've had in the last few days,' he says nonchalantly, looking around at Mr Bookmaker who, after paying Scotty, has been bailed up by a punter in the restaurant who seems to semi-know him.

'See you next time, sportsman.' The security guy winks at Jesse as he walks off to rescue Paris and the girls. They are trapped for a minute at the top of the stairs while the bookmaker tries to deal with his new best friend, which means they are standing right next to Vinnie, who has done his best to avoid contact with the whole crew up until this point.

'Vinnie!' the young bookie shouts in desperation.

'Yeah, that's right,' Vinnie responds. 'Don't bother booking a table or anything, Tom.' And really, anyone who even remotely knows Vinnie Rae knows that this is a potentially explosive situation.

'Vinnie, I'm sorry, mate. I couldn't call, the press are all over us and I just couldn't . . .' Tom pleads.

'Do I look like the fucking paparazzi, mate?'

Then Paris intervenes. 'Paris Hilton,' she says, holding out her hand.

'Vinnie Rae,' Vinnie replies, getting up from his chair and shaking her hand. 'How was lunch?'

'Great!' says Paris.

'So nice,' chime in the rest of the girls.

'It was definitely the best meal we've had in Australia,' Paris adds, as the security guys start moving things along.

'Glad you enjoyed it,' Vinnie replies, as one of the security guys says, 'Got to go. Now!' He holds up his phone, as if we're all in a movie.

'Thanks so much for everything,' Paris calls to Vinnie as she skips down the stairs with Nicky and the girls, the smell of perfume wafting back to hit the kitchen.

Tom wraps his arm around Vinnie and guides him down the stairs as the girls pile into a car that screeches into the drive. Heads are turning everywhere, from punters trying to get a park on Marine Parade, to guests in the hotel, to passersby on their way to the beach. It's like this small moment of chaos has been suppressed up until now, and at the point of departure people are keen to shake it up, say what they always wanted to say, be what they always wanted to be. Famous people are weird like that. We generally have a celebrity of some description at Rae's, either staying in the hotel or dining, but there's no doubt there's been something different about Paris Hilton. It's like she really is the centre of something in this particular cultural moment, and when she leaves the people she waves back to lack direction for a beat as if, now she's gone, everyone's lives are somehow a little less meaningful.

The car with the girls inside screeches back out of the driveway and roars down Marine Parade. Another car pulls into the driveway. The security guys pile into that car, then wait while Tom tries to smooth things over with Vinnie. But Vinnie is not easy to win over. He doesn't give a fuck what the other punters in the restaurant think of him or the staff or anyone else; he's the host and owner of Rae's of Watego's and Tom got it wrong when he thought it would be a good idea to dine at Rae's and not tell Vinnie they were coming.

Despite not being able to hear what Vinnie is telling him, it's obvious the guy is getting a dressing-down. Eventually Tom hangs his head, nods in agreement with everything Vinnie is saying, then slinks off into the waiting car.

Vinnie bounds back up the stairs at Rae's and takes his place again at the table with Jackie. Order is restored. Vinnie's presence fills the celebrity vacuum that Paris Hilton has left. And as Vinnie might say, 'Who the fuck is Paris Hilton anyway?'

'You ready for the fries, Chef?' Choc asks.

'Fuck yeah,' I reply, and clap twice for service. 'Let's get Vinnie's food out, ladies.'

'Salad's up, Chef,' Jesse says.

'Fries in one minute, Chef,' Choc tells me.

'Sodapop, you lazy dishwashing shit-for-brains, give me a hand to plate up these dishes,' I call down to Soda, who desperately needs a break from the galley. 'Choc, take over on the dishes for ten minutes.'

'Yes, Chef.'

'What do you want me to do, Chef?' Soda asks.

'Wok me up a fish of the day pot and shine up two plates,' I instruct.

Soda fires the wok up straight away, turns on the water that keeps the surface of the wok station cool, lightly oils the top of the wok and then dumps the vegetable pot into the instantly hot copper bowl.

I admire the way that all the boys in my kitchen have a certain confidence at the wok. I've worked hard to ensure they're all comfortable with its peculiar ways. To see Soda now, having not been anywhere near the wok for a week, rip into it like he owns a street stall in Thailand is satisfying.

'Vinnie's lunch ready, Chef?' Scotty asks.

'Hang about, mate,' I tell him. 'C'mon, Soda, get those plates down and shine the fuckers. I'm ready on the protein.'

My portion of beef and extra-small portion of fish are resting on the protein tray. I could have done the plates and sides myself but Soda was fading down in the galley and I wanted to snap him out of dishwasher land and into service.

'Yes, Chef,' responds Soda, who is moving like a professional chef ought to move. In the next half a minute he has the plates polished, the vegetables for the fish cooked to perfection and spooned neatly onto one of the plates with just the right amount of wok sauce oozing out from under them. Then he salts the fries and pours them into a sparkling white bowl set with creased white paper.

'I think we might let Soda spend some time down here on woks tonight,' I tell Jesse and Choc.

'Yes, Chef,' they respond, familiar with the routine of mixing up positions in order to share around time spent at the dishwasher.

'You reckon we can afford a dishie tonight, Chef?' Jesse asks facetiously.

'Only if you're paying for it, Jesse,' I inform him.

'Yeah, I'll pay if I don't have to do any dishes,' Jesse says.

'We're obviously paying Jesse far too much money, Chef,' Scotty puts in.

'I think he was going to pay with sexual favours, Scotty,' I say.

'Where's my fucking lunch, you clowns?' Vinnie leans into the kitchen.

'Coming up now, Chef,' I tell him.

'You fucking morons can't cook steak anyway. Mr Fucking Carpetbag Steak here . . .' Vinnie goes on with it, taking the piss out of me in front of the boys, something he is fond of doing when things go well: pull the glory out from under head chef in order that the rest of the crew get to feel a little less like the kitchen scum they really are.

'You want me to tuck a few oysters into your steak, Vinnie?' I ask, giving it back to him as much as I am able to without ending up on my knees.

'Fucking oysters . . . you would too. That's what they did in the seventies, wasn't it? What are you doing, Scotty? Mr Fucking Technology! Can't use a phone, can't phone a friend. You're fucking hopeless, mate,' Vinnie says, warming to the task of taking Scotty apart, limb by limb. He has obviously swallowed a quick half-bottle of

141

wine and is starting to get a shine on. His mojo would appear to be flooding back through his system, his confidence returned, after being temporarily thrown off-balance by the whole Paris Hilton thing. Now it's time to pull everyone down a few pegs, get their minds back on the job.

Scotty grabs the plates off the pass and nods at Vinnie, all business. 'You ready for this?' Scotty asks.

'Of course I'm fucking ready. I've been ready for half an hour, you clown. Fucking Jackie's lost two pounds just waiting for her . . . oh, that's very nice, Chef.' Vinnie laughs when he sees the size of Jackie's piece of fish. 'Now I've got to listen to her for the next hour while she whines on about how small the portions are at Rae's.'

'Food costs are killing us, Vinnie,' I suggest as a possible argument.

'Mate, she saw all the figures the other night,' Vinnie sighs. 'I got too pissed to put the paperwork away and she went through everything.' He laughs again. 'She knows it's you clowns that are costing me all the fucking money.'

'Jesse wants to know if we can have a kitchen hand tonight, Vinnie,' I call after him as he walks back out to the restaurant.

'You're on dishes tonight, Jesse. Fucking dishwasher . . .' Vinnie shakes his head, like he can't believe what he just heard. 'There's four of you idiots in the kitchen and you want a kitchen porter as well.'

'Thanks, Chef.' Jesse nods to me from over in larder as Vinnie disappears from view.

'I'm here for you, Jesse,' I tell him.

'Where's Vinnie's fucking mustard?' Scotty is back, and he sounds pissed off.

'Settle down, mate. C'mon, Choc, just because you're on dishes doesn't mean you can drop the ball over here, mate.'

'Sorry, Chef,' says Choc, and he grabs the hot English mustard from the stand-up fridge.

'Jackie's whingeing about her fish,' Scotty adds.

'Did you tell her the food costs are killing us?' I ask.

'Vinnie did,' Scotty says, and all the chefs laugh.

Scotty grabs the mustard and runs back to the restaurant.

'He's stressed,' I observe.

'He knows what's coming,' Jesse says.

'Yes, he does,' I acknowledge. 'And I don't want to miss it.'

21

I was working at a cafe in Coogee when Alice and I started going out. It was a time of new beginnings for us, and endings for a number of people we knew. In many ways, things got off to an overly serious start; like, I don't actually know you that well but here we are at another funeral. In fact, we weren't sufficiently close to go to all the different funerals together—it would have been disrespectful to our families—but we lived through the various grieving processes and got to see how each other ticked.

A couple of junkie mates and my little brother died, as did assorted grandparents and Alice's previous boyfriend, all in the first six months of going out. It was an emotionally complex time where we kept getting tossed between the highs of falling in love and the lows of dealing with an impossibly long procession of deaths.

During that time, I'd start work at six each morning in the cafe and begin the day by baking off breads, cakes and whatever specials needed to get done for lunch. At about seven Alice would come in to see me and grab a pastry and a coffee before going off to uni. Each day I would forage and search for some new ingredient to use in the baking to impress her. And our nights together merged into one long dream where my mission was always the same: to create some magic flavour that would somehow elevate Alice out of the sadness which was everywhere around us at that time and seemed impossible to escape.

What I realise now and didn't then is that it's unusual for two people to have quite such complicated histories, quite so young. Most evenings we'd spend our time going over old ground; me compelled to tell her my ridiculous secrets before she somehow discovered them for herself, and Alice eventually letting me into her secret world and hidden stories, which in their telling seemed to clutch and claw and catch and slowly pull her down.

In order to lure her back to the surface I cooked. My recipes were all the same, involving gas fires and heated pots, oils and spices and garlic and time. While potions boiled and bubbled, I would set the table with plates and bowls and knives and forks and candles and spoons and cups and wait. Slowly I would bring my sweet love home, up from the icy depths, and we'd eat.

I worked in a lot of average kitchens in the early days of our relationship. My ambition at the time had nothing to do with a career in fine dining or write-ups in the newspaper or pats on the back from chefs much better than me. And Alice wasn't interested in marrying a workaholic cook or famous chef. She wanted to spend her life with a human being: someone she could talk to and share things with; someone who would look after the kids and feed the pets and take out the rubbish and listen.

As the years rolled away and the kids came, we were forced to make do with fate's hand. And as my energies became once more focused on larger kitchens with brigades of chefs and job descriptions that required obsessive attention to every little detail, it was her turn to listen to my stories. How from nine till noon I would be checking off deliveries and prepping my section; how I'd rotate everything in the coolroom to keep a handle on what supplies were needed. How each chef had to have their section ready for service: fresh sauce, protein, herbs, garnishes, oils, seasoning. And how each chef had to know how many serves they had of everything they were responsible for cooking. How when the lunch bell rang at midday, it was all hands on deck.

At three pm lunch service would end and each chef would break down their section and clean it up and start a prep list for service that night, the maître d' yelling booking updates into the kitchen every time the phone rang. I told Alice about how I determined which chef would cook a staff meal on any given night; how if there was a section that wasn't ready for service they would be left alone to get it boxed. How after a quick dinner and the six o'clock call and last-minute preparations and adjustments the adrenaline would surge at the sound of the first order clicking through the docket machine. And I'd tell her how, when I called my first check down the line, my voice would always be a little tight, like until I'd heard the three or four or five chefs on the line all call back, 'Yes, Chef' or, 'Oui, Chef', I was never sure I wasn't alone.

It takes a team effort to fend off the chaos of a busy lunch or dinner service in a half-decent restaurant. Kitchen life is a social event in restaurants that require a brigade of chefs to function. It becomes normal to end up spending more time with grungy, blood-splattered chefs and kitchen porters than at home with loved ones. Marriages and partnerships bend and twist from the endless heat and pressure. Some find ways to adapt and mould or cope. Some buckle beyond repair.

I have been fortunate over the last fifteen years in that one look from Alice can always bring me undone. A particular mood or cool stare will break the spell of the most manic situation. Not that she does it often. Like most people we negotiate the complexities of life, but if I lose focus for too long and forget what really matters, she'll say the word and I'll collect my knives and walk away.

The photos she's been sending me lately are a warning bell. There's still a playfulness about them; it might amount to nothing. But along with her efforts in the garden and the heatwave that hangs over everything, things might also erupt in any number of ways. All of which will bring about the end of things for me at Rae's and a return to her, and us, and our most treasured recipes.

22

Returning to Balmain a couple of years after having worked at Sorrentino's was a strange experience. I certainly hadn't plotted my return via Desperate Hour at Kings Cross, but given it had happened my sole responsibility was to put all that out of my mind and start again. The thing I was most happy about was that Sorrentino's had disappeared from the neighbourhood. Last I'd heard, Doug had sold the business after taking the whole branding thing too far down-market. Which was liberating for me; it meant an aspect of my past had been erased. This also meant I could walk down the street without crossing the road or ducking under umbrellas in the sun. I owed Doug and the Italians some money and no end of goodwill, but I was a little short on both.

I went to a couple of interviews in the neighbourhood and ended up taking a job that was all about the money. It was another pasta joint and incredibly busy. The chef-owner had just sold the business and part of closing the deal was that they had to find someone who could do the four days he worked in a similar fashion to him. No one was too worried about what it might cost because the job was difficult. The kitchen was so small it made most domestic settings look five-star. Physically, there was only enough space for a chef and a kitchen hand. The joint sat just twenty-five people but ninety percent of the trade was takeaway. The phone would start ringing around five thirty and wouldn't stop until nine. It was insane; someone was employed just to answer the phone and write up orders.

Each pasta dish was individually cooked in a frypan, which was different to the Barracks and the Pasta Man in that there was no pasta sink and pots of sauce. It was à la carte, which meant if we did two hundred covers during a service, there were two hundred frypans to clean and bucket-loads of *mise en place* to prepare. I had a large pot of water at my feet where I dropped the pans after I plated up a dish. As I ran out of clean pans, I would rinse off the dirty ones in the pot and start again. As a system it was rudimentary. The original owners had set up shop in a Victorian terrace on Darling Street and assumed they'd make a living. What they ended up making, in the five years they owned it before selling, was a small fortune.

They'd tried a few people out before I started at Darling Street and none of them had stuck, which meant no one was expecting me to either. But they weren't to know how desperate I was, and after doing a week and proving I had the chops for the job, I asked for a grand a week and they decided to pay. It was a lot of money back in the day and the request didn't endear me to the new owners. But on the upside, it got the old owners out, the new owners in, and if they wanted to think of me as the transition guy, well, fine; I'd take the money now and move on later. Same as it ever was.

The days were long. I started at eight in the morning and went through until ten or eleven at night, four days in a row. Every morning I had to start doing pastry section, which meant making one or more of the five dessert items on the menu. Then I would have to get the pots of sauce on and start cooking off pasta. It wasn't just multi-tasking; it was an utter shit-fight every sunrise. I had never seen so much food produced out of such a tiny space. And the reason they didn't mind paying someone so much money was that the job was basically one person doing all the sections of a busy little cafe-cum-restaurant. If the physical space had room for two or three chefs they would have employed more people, but it didn't and as the joint got busier and busier, they had just adapted the space to cope with the extra workload.

Initially things went really well. Just like in every other place I'd ever worked, they loved me and I shut up and did the job. I was enjoying being on the pans in such a dynamic way; very few places get to use frypans with anything like the rapid-fire way we did at Darling Street. And it was rewarding to be able to survive one shift let alone a week. The main stress of the job was turning up each morning and literally having to start over, prepping everything from scratch before the phones started ringing. It was intense but it did keep my mind off other, less productive pursuits.

★★★

After a few weeks at Darling Street I had some cash behind me and had spent enough time away from Kings Cross to imagine things hadn't gone quite so badly last time I was up there. The desperate hour after the bus trip from Brisbane, although only a few weeks ago, had been filed away somewhere deep and very dark. You might even say I was on top of things. No one thought I'd be able to do the job and yet here I was, carving it up. I'd improved things, tweaked systems and got it running smoother. And pretty soon the three days off I had each week started to feel like an opportunity rather than a window of respite. So one night, after my fourteen-hour Sunday shift, I caught a cab up to the Cross and did the business.

Because I'd ripped off one of the working girls during my Newtown days I was always a little careful when I revisited the Golden Mile. One thing that worked in my favour was the fact that the Cross is a very busy and dynamic place. The names and faces change pretty regularly even if the song stays the same. I imagine they're still playing Tina Turner's 'Private Dancer' in a few of the clubs. Many people, for a multitude of reasons, are called to the Cross and everyone gets a speaking part straight off the bat. It's an egalitarian cultural space and if you have the necessary moves to last a few weeks . . . well, you've probably earned a rest somewhere quiet. And even if there are bars on the windows when you get to that restful place, it's going to be a relief after putting in such a physically demanding performance.

So the odds of being recognised in Kings Cross for my one lousy crime against the working class were strictly for the speculator. But if anyone had taken the hundred-to-one on that particular evening they would've been rolled in clover, for as I was walking up one of the laneways towards the main strip someone came out of the shadows and yelled, 'Hey!'

I didn't even bother turning. I was getting on and I figured the distraction wasn't any of my business. But when a burly little gangster grabbed me by the shoulder and spun me around, I saw the girl I'd slipped the five dollars to before running off with her fifty dollars worth of smack.

I didn't feel like a villain, though. I was scared. Perhaps never more scared in my life than in the moment when our eyes met again. The thing about using smack is that the time between tastes doesn't actually exist when you're using. It feels like it does when it's happening, when you're working away, on the straight and narrow. But it's an illusion, like a field of potential that your mind recalls in the moments when you're putting your next shot away; like déjà vu. It's like the time between ripping off a prostitute some months ago and the present, which finds her boyfriend holding on to my arm, is no time at all. It could have been yesterday, and as far as the angry little chimpanzee squeezing the sinew of my shoulder is concerned, it was. And the chimp, who had been let out of his cage for a brief reign of terror and pain, was in his element. He wasn't in jail or eating scraps out of a bin or taking it up the arse in some shithouse work-for-the-dole scheme. Right now, he was the fucking man.

'You dirty little tip-rat.'

'That's him, Joey. That's the little cunt.'

'You fucking little cunt.'

'Five fucking dollars he gave me.'

'You cheeky little cunt.'

And soon I was going to have to start speaking, but before I could Joey started pushing me back down the dark laneway, away from the neon glow of the strip, away from a taste or a tickle or a fix, and into darkness where these things lie.

'Open the fucking boot, Betty,' said Joey, fumbling around with his keys.

And I propped and pivoted, hardened the fuck up.

'Fuck off, cunt. It was only a fucking tickle.'

'Yeah, but you admit ripping Betty off, you little cunt.'

Bang! He clocked me in the side of the head. And I was expecting that; I was happy enough getting a touch-up, but I wasn't hopping into any fucking boot. Not conscious or alive, anyway.

'Don't fucking play with him, Joey. Get him in the fucking boot and shoot the little cunt.'

'Oh yeah, right, you old slut. You're gonna shoot a bloke for half a fucking stepped-on shot,' I said, full of indignant bravado.

'That wasn't stepped on. That was off-the-fucking-boat fresh, you little cunt.'

'Open the fucking boot, Betty. Don't just stand there yelling and screaming.'

'Wait a fucking minute. I'll fix you up. I'm sorry, all right? I fucked up but here.' I reached into my pocket.

And the whole time he was dragging me down the street I'd been doing the sums on how much was in this pocket and how much was in that pocket; what it was going to cost me, with interest, to shut the door on this unfortunate youthful misadventure.

'Two hundred fucking dollars doesn't cover it, cunt. You can't go running around ripping off hard-working girls and expect to get away with paying a few bob interest.'

'Some of that interest is mine, Joey,' old put-upon Betty whined in the background.

Joey spun around and backhanded her across the face. 'Shut up, you fucking idiot. If I want to hear from you I'll whistle.'

Then Joey pushed me down onto an old bench, which like the one in Newtown was riddled with graffitied histories. It was scary how little time seemed to have passed between benches; how in Newtown I'd leapt off one and run down the stairs to the train station and then alighted at Kings Cross and ripped off Betty. And it wasn't like I hadn't paid my dues in the meantime for that most despicable of crimes. Fuck me, life had caught up with me in other ways but . . . well, now probably wasn't the time to indulge in any of that.

'Empty out your pockets,' said Joey, looking around as he pulled back hard on my collar, choking me further down onto the seat.

'Go easy. It was a fucking tickle, you cunt,' I managed to cough out.

And Joey popped my lip and bent back one of my top teeth. Which seemed to give way pretty easy. Maybe I wasn't getting enough calcium.

'All right! All right, you fucking pricks.'

And now it was my time for a little show-and-fucking-tell. I ripped his arm off me and stood up, angry, making a scene as I emptied out my pockets.

'Why don't you fucking rob me blind, you cunts? Here you fucking go. Take everything I fucking got . . . take the fucking . . .'

And as I'm tipping coins and cash into the gutter, a police car squirts out a short siren.

And faster than a gutter-rat, Betty scooped the eighty or ninety dollars off the road and scurried into the shadows. Joey was already gone; he was up two hundred and didn't have to rely on Betty to come good for another couple of hours. And me . . . I stayed and chatted with the cops about the unfortunates who just robbed me. A young bloke on his way to a club; a young bloke with a busted lip and a sore head who can't remember what anyone looked like or sounded like or even what they wanted other than his money. And no, thanks for the opportunity, but I didn't want to make a statement.

I'd been at Darling Street for a few weeks and wasn't really paying rent at my brother's house, so I still had plenty of cash and managed to score that night. And to ease the pain I bought a weight rather than a tickle, with all the good intentions of any junkie at the start of another habit who buys a weight, telling myself it would last a few days. The imagined upside was that I wouldn't have to race back up to Kings Cross to score for at least a week. That was the theory anyway. Frankly, I wasn't keen on another visit any time soon, even though I couldn't see

Joey staying out of prison for longer than another forty-eight hours. Joey had that hungry look, the one that was under no illusions; the one I had in Newtown and was keen to avoid again.

Living in a garage which belonged to my brother and his family who lived upstairs did present some problems, the first of which was that there was no toilet in my corner of the world, and to get around this problem I had taken to pissing in empty alcohol bottles. On rainy nights I'd slip outside and empty the full bottles of urine into the rain-filled gutter. But given the vagaries of the weather, the times between rainy nights got so stretched for a while there that the joint started to smell and they had kids and were good hard-working people, so I cut a deal and moved out.

I'd always liked Annandale. It was quiet and leafy and had some great little continental pockets without being culturally overwhelming for a poor white renter. So I optimistically signed a six-month lease on a four-bedroom terrace which ate up about half my pay. I really felt like I needed some space and, besides, I thought I'd be able to let some rooms out to help pay the rent. I also wanted to limit what I could do with the money I was earning by spending as much as I could on things like rent, food, motorbikes and clothes before I spent money on drugs. And it was a noble plan. But you know what happens to the best-laid plans . . .

23

It's three thirty in the afternoon and lunch service has just finished at Rae's. The restaurant is half full of guests lingering over unfinished bottles of wine, petits fours and coffee. At this stage of the afternoon most people have very little else to do if they're dining in Byron Bay. And that's because they're all on holidays. Guests don't usually have to run off to work or a pressing business engagement or very much else. So they sit and stare out at the view which, at this point in the day, is all sunburnt tourists, sand-covered children dragging boogie boards back to cars and the spectacle of breasts, butts and bikinis.

Vinnie and Jackie look to be settling in for a cracking afternoon session. Some of the other guests have pulled chairs over to their table, and Vinnie is holding court with stories about Watego's, Paris Hilton and, quite possibly, how hard it is to make a buck these days.

In the kitchen it's all soap suds and steel wool, hot-water hoses and Firedog. Firedog is the brand name of a chemical concoction that a lot of contemporary kitchens store beneath their sink. To suggest it's a grease-cutter would not adequately prepare a person for the skin-peeling, eye-burning, tear-inducing vapour that leaps out of the keg whenever the lid is twisted off. We have songs about Firedog in our kitchen; they are generally sung in a high-pitched voice to indicate the ball-shrinking, fear-inducing quality of the compound. Basically, everyone is scared of the effect it has on the human body, but in awe of what it does to a greasy kitchen. Just the sound of its name is an ominous threat: the coiled spring of kitchen cleaners.

And despite Jesse not being in a joke-cracking mood today, he still thinks he might have a bit of fun with the Firedog. He flicks a few drops at Soda, who immediately drops what he's doing and rushes Jesse, taking hold of his throat.

'You're a fucking idiot,' Soda spits.

'Hey!' I yell at them, not bothering to get too worked up. 'Don't be a fuckhead all your life, Jesse.'

Soda lets go of Jesse's throat with a push that throws Jesse back into the white-tiled wall.

Jesse is laughing like it's all a great joke. 'You cunts need to loosen the fuck up,' he says, but it's obvious that Jesse is the one among us who's most uptight.

Soda looks hurt, like it kills him to have to discipline the guy he looks up to most in life. His easy grin has set into a *what the fuck are you doing?* expression.

'Jesse, I don't know what you're problem is, mate . . . I hope it's just this moving house thing, but you'd better sort yourself out. In fact, fuck off now and do whatever you've got to do so you can get back in time to box your section. You're on larder again tonight. Soda, you're

doing woks like we said and Choc, you're doing everything else, all right?'

'Yes, Chef,' they shout.

'So I can go now?' Jesse asks.

'Yeah. Fuck off. We'll finish cleaning the place up,
but Jesse—get your head screwed on for tonight. Really,
you guys, we're fucking close, all right? Everyone's got a
day off coming up. Just keep your shit together and your
section boxed and we're going to make it out of this high
season and fucking heatwave and into surfing paradise.
Okay?' I half threaten, half implore them.

'Yes, Chef,' they all respond.

'Cop ya,' Jesse says as he rips off his apron and walks
out of the kitchen.

'Four o'clock, Jesse!' I call after him.

But Jesse just winks at me as he passes the bar and
waves back like, *I'm free!*

Soda looks cut. He has never spoken ill of Jesse behind
his back before and it's not my place to start running him
down to make Soda feel any better about things.

'You guys . . .' I say, shaking my head. And I want
to yell at Soda to get out: leave Jesse and us behind and
jump a train and see where it leads or hang a thumb out
by the road. Soda's too spirited for the grease and grime
of the kitchen galley, too good-looking and easy-going
for the sweat and stress and heartaches of kitchen life. And
I'm scared that if he doesn't get out soon, get out into the
sunshine, which is where a kid like Soda belongs, then
he's going to be stuck inside the fluorescent and stainless-
steel world of restaurant kitchens until it's too late and
he's just like one of us.

159

And then Soda stops what he's doing and kicks out at some empty boxes. 'Jesse's a fuckwit.'

'A giant, herpes-ridden, cockhead fuckwit,' I say, going on with it.

'Yeah! Take that, Jesse!' Scotty chimes in as he dumps a pile of dirty plates onto the waiters' station.

'How's Vinnie?' I ask.

'He says you still can't cook a steak, Chef, but the salad's finally how he likes it,' Scotty says.

'Tell him I said get fucked and Paris Hilton loves everything I do.'

'He hates Paris Hilton. Reckons she can't act and should have continued with her online career,' Scotty says.

'Oh, that actually hurts. I've got half a chubby that says Paris had a thing for me . . . Really, she was vibing me through the walls. Vinnie's just upset. He's always had a thing for Paris—he was talking about her a few days ago when she was in the Sydney papers,' I tell Scotty.

'He's changed, Chef,' Scotty informs me as he walks back out to the restaurant.

'It's you that's changed, Scotty. And I liked you better before,' I call after him.

Soda rips up the empty boxes and flattens them out, stamping them into a neat pile beneath the sink.

'You want me to get the wok section set up for tonight, Chef?' he asks.

'Yeah, mate,' I say, relieved that he has come through, that for the sake of service tonight he hasn't run away. 'Pull everything out of your reach-in fridge; clean it, polish it, re-box everything and do a prep list, okay?

I also want you to go out to the coolroom and tidy up your section there and do me an order for tomorrow.'

'Yes, Chef,' Soda replies, and begins pulling everything out of the reach-in service fridge.

'And Choc, you can do the same on pastry section. Get everything ready down there because we're going to be slammed again tonight. I'm going to try to organise a kitchen hand, fuck what Vinnie says, because there's no way we can get this place clean by the end of service for the crew tomorrow,' I say to the boys. 'I want the kitchen spotless for our fearless sous-chef tomorrow, or it's your balls he's going to nibble on,' I remind Soda. 'And don't tell me you like it when he does that.'

Joseph is the sous-chef at Rae's and he's running the show tomorrow while Jesse and I take a day off. Joseph is from Trinidad and while he's as cool as everyone else from Trini, he's also a clean freak and demands nothing less than I would expect from a sous-chef. Which is to say, at the end of our run in the kitchen, we leave it how we want to find it when we start back on. And even if Jesse and I are only getting one day off, it is still our responsibility to leave the place clean and boxed, meaning there's a sufficient quantity of *mise en place* to get underway in the morning, as well as an accurate list of jobs that need to be done, all set out in order of importance. It is also our responsibility to make sure that the ordering is accurate so that the produce that turns up tomorrow is exactly what the boys need. You don't leave the next crew in the shit. And they're no longer crew if they leave me there. It's a reciprocal thing and when everyone is looking after everyone else, as much as it is possible to do so during such a busy time, the crew has a decent chance of sticking together for more than a few weeks.

Getting a crew together in any kitchen is always the most difficult aspect of being a head chef. There's a particular chemistry that has to unfold between people in order for the line to run smoothly. And there seems to be no sure way of getting that to happen; it just does through natural attrition and time. When a position comes up that you can't fill through word of mouth, you advertise and try chefs out until you find one that sticks. So many things have to gel in order for a person to both fit in with the existing crew and for the crew to accept that new person that to try and second-guess the process or work out some formula is impossible.

The particular problem with finding chefs in Byron Bay is that, because it's a tourist destination, many chefs only stay in town for short periods of time. In Sydney or Melbourne or any other city where there's a critical mass, a head chef can get a crew together that might stay as a team for several years. And that crew might hold tough through several restaurants, in different suburbs, with various menus. They all come to an end at some point, though, and when they do—usually because the sous-chef wants to be a head chef or the chef de partie wants to be the sous-chef—the only way to fill the void is with a new team player.

Our current crew at Rae's has been going strong for two and a half years but the strain is beginning to show. Jesse has already run away to Sydney with his girlfriend to hit the high notes of fine dining in the big city, only to return to Byron minus his girlfriend and beg for his job back. He was fortunate because, during the time he was gone, we'd tried out half a dozen chefs for his job and none of them had worked out. Every kitchen has a particular culture, a set of quirks that make each of them a little different. One new chef might not like the roster, another one the pay, another one his apprentice.

Jesse, Choc, Soda, Joseph and myself came together through word of mouth and good luck. Jesse and Soda came as a package, both being local boys who had worked together in a number of other restaurants around town. Jesse had decided he wanted to cook modern Thai and since we were the best shop in town doing that cuisine, he started at the top. Jesse's résumé indicated two things: that he was someone who moved around a lot, and that he had very few computer skills. Most chefs these days fill out their résumé with so much clutter that it takes ten minutes to work out what's bullshit and what's real. Jesse's CV didn't suffer from such wasted effort. As such, he got a trial and after about an hour I offered him the job. A few days later, after he'd settled in and I'd established just how good he was, Soda started coming in to work with him. Initially Soda would just turn up late in the shift and help out on dishes in order to get Jesse out of the place. Then someone else left and Soda joined the crew and I haven't been able to get rid of them since.

Joseph and Choc came with the job. Joseph was the sous-chef for the last head chef and was happy enough to stay on when I started. Choc was indentured as an apprentice to Vinnie and he was solid from the start. Always polite and undemanding, my biggest concern was that he didn't really appreciate that Rae's was actually quite a weird place to work rather than the standard. Don't get me wrong, everywhere is weird in some way, it's just that it was obvious Choc was going to benefit enormously from gaining experience in a variety of commercial kitchens.

When the team that's been together for a long time starts to crumble it can be quite distressing. Timing is critical in terms of collapse. One of the biggest upsides to working in hospitality, though, is that there's always another job out there. I've become accustomed to moving on and running a different kitchen with a whole new crew when things turn to shit. Maybe I'll take one player from the old kitchen, someone who hasn't burnt out yet and is keen to be promoted into a better job in the new kitchen, or maybe I'll just wipe the slate clean and start fresh. What's happening at Rae's now is that the strain is beginning to show during what is the peak of our high season.

The two-week period from Christmas Day through to about the tenth of January is the busiest time in the hospitality industry throughout the Western world. The way our calendar is set makes these two weeks a virtual blackout zone in the high-rise buildings of most large English-speaking cities of the world. It is a time where people escape back to family and friends, beachside villas and country retreats. It's a time to relax, unwind and enjoy the spoils of hospitality. Unless you're a chef.

If you're a chef, you'll be working in one of those seaside villas or country retreats. And chances are you'll be so busy that the possibility of your crew falling apart is high. Minor personality clashes become all-out war under so much stress; petty resentments boil over into screaming matches and knife throwing. And if your crew is starting to fray around the edges, like ours is, the whole thing can go to shit during one bad service. Which is why I'm trying to nurse the younger boys through this war zone. It's not that they're unaware that everyone's nerves are frayed and tensions are high, it's simply that they have done less high seasons than the older crew and are more likely to snap under the pressure.

After a person has been a chef for a period of time—and I think that period of time is different for different people—they come to accept that the busy, intense times of kitchen life are simply part of the game rather than something to try and avoid or get worked up about. But there's no other way to arrive at that understanding other than to go through the jungle enough times to realise you're going to come out the other side. Eventually, what becomes important is not just getting out the other side, but travelling through with a little style and grace.

For Jesse, that's not going to happen this year. He's on a very slippery slope, and even if he wants to stop or slow down he can't. The brakes are failing and the steepness of the descent is too much for him to handle with anything that remotely resembles self-respect. And, really, that's okay, I've been there. It's his capacity to spring back from a fucked-up landing that I'm worried about, particularly since he's already failed one attempt to leave. The reality is, even if we can manage to get through the next few weeks, the team is going to fall apart not long after that. No one wants it to, but everyone can see it coming. And it's that inevitability that seems to be haunting everything we do. No one quite knows how it's going to end, what event will act as the catalyst that splinters our little group.

The thing that will stay the same at Rae's is Vinnie. It's his name that hangs over the door. He's the common factor among all the kitchen crews that have passed through the joint over the last fifteen years and it's his energy and enthusiasm that maintains a sense of continuity about the place. And I haven't dismissed the idea of sacking Jesse and getting a new chef de partie—that's what I'd normally do—but this year I'm physically feeling things a little more than I'd like to, and I'm struggling to ramp up the energy and enthusiasm that running a five-star restaurant requires.

I know Alice is getting tired of the high seasons at Rae's. And there are other options. As I flicked through the positions vacant in the local paper last week, I became fixated on an ad placed by a small restaurant in town that's seeking a new head chef. And what interested me most about that job is the fact that the restaurant is a dinner joint: they don't open for lunch or breakfast or have room service to worry about. The idea of starting work around two in the afternoon, six days a week, has become like a sweet dream I can't escape. Particularly at eight in the morning when the kids are jumping all over me, and instead of enjoying the experience I find it a struggle to maintain my equanimity. While I'm covered in glory by working at Rae's, the cost is killing me. And though the money is good—at least thirty grand a year more than I'd be getting at the dinner joint in town— there comes a time when it's never enough.

The equation in terms of pay for a head chef works in such a way that the lower down the food chain a chef goes the more control they have over their hours, but the less pay they take home. And it works that way because to work in an environment that puts a premium on everything you do, from the quality of the produce to the type of crockery you use, to the tone of the service, is inspiring. The attention to detail and the customers' expectations in a fine-dining scene ensures a certain level of both adrenaline and sophistication that becomes intoxicating. The problem is that unless you own the restaurant and can occasionally step back from the madness, the obsessive attention to every little detail and the need for single-minded perfection means that life becomes too narrow.

'Vinnie wants some canapés for his table of friends, Chef,' Scotty calls into the kitchen. And Scotty knows the kitchen is closed. He understands we've packed the lunch service away and we're in the process of scrubbing down and getting ready for dinner. And he knows because, like me, he's seen it all before.

'Just something simple,' I suggest, mimicking Vinnie. 'Some prawns, a few oysters and scallops, maybe a sweet pork and papaya salad?'

'You're all over it, Chef,' Scotty replies. 'Might be best to keep things extra-simple, though, and just do a nice, big, fresh seafood platter.' He walks out.

Soda and Choc have stopped what they're doing and are looking at me, soapy scourers in hand, sections in chaos, like *you can't be fucking serious*.

'One seafood platter, boys,' I call.

'Yes, Chef,' they reply, their enthusiasm for the task buried somewhere so deep it struggles for breath.

'And no fucking short cuts,' I add. 'This is for the boss. I want every little thing perfect, okay?'

'Yes, Chef,' they repeat, still subdued.

'Don't fuck with me, men. Get cracking!' I say, clapping my hands. And that's all it takes to pick the boys up. Really, I'm surprised how well these two are responding. They actually give me some faith that if I do choose to stay on at Rae's, all I really have to do is get rid of Jesse and find some fresh energy for his section. Why throw the whole thing away? I've worked hard to get the restaurant where it is, and other than Jesse the crew is strong.

'Fuck this. I need a smoke.' And just like that, Soda bombs my daydream.

Choc and I watch as Soda walks out past the bar, his head hung low, pulling a crumpled pack of Winfield Reds from his pocket. And I say nothing, picturing instead Soda leaping up onto a moving train.

'It's you and me, old mate,' I say to Choc.

'Yes, Chef,' replies Choc.

'I'll do the bugs and the prawns and the fish, you get the salads started and crack that crab open.'

'Yes, Chef.'

If it were any other time of year, I'd be forced to sack Soda—and Jesse—today! But because I can't, and because they know I can't, I have to suck it up as Soda stomps up the wooden hallway that runs beside the kitchen.

'What's his problem?' Choc wants to know.

'Well,' I say, 'I think he's probably just a young, pussy-whipped pain in the arse who can't stand the heat. I think that, because of Jesse, this crew is probably going to fall to shit sometime soon and there's not much I can do to stop that happening.'

'Everyone's just stressed out, Chef,' Choc assures me.

'Mate,' I say, 'everyone just seems over it this year. We've had a pretty good run, and we need to see the season out, but it might just be time to fuck this puppy.'

'Which puppy is that, Chef?' Scotty calls out as he dumps more dirty coffee cups onto the crowded waiters' station.

'Fucking stack those plates, Scotty, or the whole thing's going to crash and burn,' I tell him.

'Which puppy are we fucking?' Scotty asks again.

'Nothing,' I tell him. 'We were just talking shit.'

'Vinnie said to hurry up on that fucking platter or he'll sack you,' Scotty adds before he walks out.

And that is just so Vinnie Rae I can't stand it. He would have seen Jesse go up the tunnel, followed soon after by Soda, and he'd know why they did. Because he's a chef, Vinnie can feel the pressure in the kitchen building, it's an intuitive thing that a chef doesn't lose— apparently—and all that experience tells him that when things are at their most critical, it's the perfect time to throw a firecracker into the middle of it all. He's an expert. Really, I've learnt everything I know about how to get the most out of people from Vinnie Rae. The problem with Vinnie's model, though, is he keeps pushing until everything does crash and burn. Not that he gives a fuck. I guess he figures that chefs are only at their best for a couple of years anyway and it's better to get fresh talent through the place every so often. Nine days out of ten I'll just sidestep Vinnie's jab, maybe even serve it back with something extra, but it seems I'm getting slower and somehow dumber.

And that's the way it works. Pretty soon, a new head chef will arrive at Rae's with a couple of his or her crew from the last place they all worked at. They'll do a new menu and deep clean the joint, the soundtrack to their labour a constant put-down of the last crew and their piece-of-shit menu. They'll whine to Vinnie about the state of the coolroom and the grease at the back of the stove and Vinnie will shake his head like, *un-fucking-believable*. And then he'll say something like, 'Have you done the dinner menu yet, Chef?'

In fact, the new head chef will sound just like me in whatever new joint I land in. And I figure the reason crews crash and burn, come and go, 'until the next gig . . .', is because the job of being a chef is intrinsically creative. Every day is a journey into the heat, colour, movement and chaos of creating a new plate of food for every single guest who arrives at our restaurant. And every time I cook a dish, it's a new dish. Things change. Cooking in a fine-dining atmosphere is not like working in McDonald's where there is no room to experiment. In here, in the heat, sweat and abuse of a busy five-star restaurant kitchen, it's a fucking circus performance each day and every night. And it's draining. Most places have their rosters better figured out than Vinnie allows, but again, it doesn't have my name over the door and the way Vinnie sees it is that, if he was head chef, he'd be in here at six o'clock every morning and he wouldn't leave until midnight when the kitchen was Firedogged to within an inch of its life.

And I don't know what it is about today—maybe it's the sight of Vinnie popping that consolation bottle of Cristal that he never got to drink with Paris, or maybe I'm just getting too old to dance to this particular beat—but I resolve that I'll phone the owner of that little dinner joint in town tomorrow and sound him out about things. Just the thought of talking about a new menu with a new boss, standing inside a different kitchen with a different array of cooking implements . . . well, it's the most inspired I've been for a few weeks.

'Salad's are up, Chef,' Choc informs me.

'Good work, Choc. They look awesome. Really, that's nice work, mate.' And I'm serious. The food is clean, fresh and alive. It looks both healthy and irresistible. Great Thai food is like that. 'Now get that platter down and polish it. And get some banana mat on it.'

'Yes, Chef.'

There's no use fighting the endgame. I could walk out myself now—and I wouldn't be the first head chef to walk out of Rae's without giving notice—but I don't want to. If I'm going to leave, I want to do so on my terms and I want a nice, long holiday before I start up somewhere else. At least a week. And at least fifty kilometres away from where I live.

'Get these bugs onto the banana mat and cut up some lime for me, Choc.'

'Yes, Chef.'

'How are the oysters?'

'Yeah, good, Chef.' Choc hands me a freshly shucked local oyster over the pass.

I slide the oyster into my mouth and can't help but agree. 'Plate me up a dozen of those little fuckers when you've done the platter.'

'Yes, Chef.'

'And fix yourself up something nice for lunch, mate. What would you like?'

'I might have a steak, Chef. If that's all right?'

'Mate,' I say with some enthusiasm. 'I know that because we work at Rae's we get the privilege of watching Vinnie's lifestyle, but every now and then, we give a dog a bone!'

'Yes, Chef,' Choc says again like the polite young man he is.

'Here's the fish and chips and the prawns. Finish that platter and I'll get our lunch underway.'

Soda walks back into the kitchen reeking of dope, his eyes a little distant.

'You joining Choc and me for lunch, Soda?' I enquire. 'We're having a nice lump of prime rib steak with a little mushroom ragu and some fries.'

'Yeah, righto, Chef,' Soda replies, and I can tell he's thinking: *That's right! Sometimes I have to eat things rather than just cook them.*

'Well, get this fucking kitchen clean,' I instruct him. 'Then we can sit down out the back by the pool and enjoy our lunch.'

'Yes, Chef!'

24

A week after I signed the lease on the terrace in Annandale, the new owners at Darling Street called me into a meeting one morning and basically let me go. I've got to say I didn't see it coming. To their credit, they paid me a couple of weeks' notice plus whatever benefits I had accrued, which amounted to quite a tidy little bundle of cash. And there was a big piece of me that was pleased to end the routine. I wasn't worried about getting more work; in the hospitality industry people come and go, restaurants open and shut, trends fly by faster all the time. If this joint decided they could find someone to do the same or better work for less money, well, good luck to them. That they went broke and shut up shop six months later was not something to celebrate.

A lot of people are cynical about themed pubs, particularly the Irish ones, and I get that, but the London Hotel was different because it'd been in Balmain for over a hundred years. And although there was some naff British stuff scattered about the place, the London was a serious suburban hotel that had recently had some serious money spent on it. They'd hired a good head chef in Andrew and the team was turning out a very smart early-nineties menu. There was a line of four chefs, and when they put an ad in the newspaper for a sous-chef to replace Gavin, Gavin was still there, which meant when I got the job, the person who knew everything about the section was able to hand it over to me in an organised manner. The team was focused, clean and busy. Andrew was constantly experimenting and changing the menu and winning new friends in both the suburb and the media. I took a pay cut after Darling Street, but given the job was for a sous-chef rather than a commis chef or chef de partie, I only dropped a couple of hundred a week, and I figured the benefits far outweighed the negatives.

I was immensely relieved to be back on a line after having been a head chef in kitchens with one or two other cooks or kitchen hands. I liked the grill section; it meant I was doing all the protein preparation and got to stand at the head of line and call the pass. Andrew took control on the two busiest shifts of the week, Friday and Saturday nights, but during the rest of the week he did sauce preparation and menu planning while I organised and cooked the pass.

The menu at the London borrowed from a cuisine that came to be labelled New British. It was lighter than a lot of the stodge that the British seem to love. New British borrowed from the Mediterranean by using olive oil rather than butter and was notable for its use of colour. It was also responsible for putting fruit back on the mains plate with things like passionfruit jus and golden apple

174

galette. A typical dish might have been something like tea-smoked salmon with baby beetroot rosti, butter beans and passionfruit jus. You can just see the colours: the orange of the salmon with the purple rosti crust and the vivid yellow sauce. You'd finish the dish with some micro-herbs or maybe some butter beans and it would be served in a heavy white bistro bowl-plate.

I still like a lot of the things I learnt at the London— even the pork-belly pie—but the thing I enjoyed most was being back on the line without the stress of running the show. I was comfortable cooking for ten or a hundred as long as the rest of the crew were ready for action, but at the end of the day I could go home safe in the knowledge that it would be Andrew stressing about tomorrow rather than me. I started to wean myself off the heroin by beginning the day with a few shots of alcohol. Each morning would see me order a short black espresso from the bar that I would turn into something more delicious with Kahlua or Johnnie Walker or a random combination of whatever else was in the kitchen's alcohol supply.

The shifts at the London were split, which is always a drag. It meant that after lunch service I would have two or three hours where, if I didn't have to work through to dinner service in order to get my section up to speed, I would have to kill the time either by sitting at the bar in another pub down the road or falling asleep in the store-room or . . . getting to know one of the waitresses. We were blessed at the London with some spectacularly well-presented waitresses who were all blind to my defects of character. Not since the Bondi Hotel had I been so in Cupid's gaze. Then something happened which changed any expectations I had about how rosy my future was beginning to look.

The new girl, who had just come back from Britain and was all milky skin and Laura Ashley, disclosed to me that she was running a habit that she just knew I would be able to help her out with. And I know blaming anyone for your problems in life is piss-weak, but Caroline . . . well, she was trouble with a capital C. In about eight days I'd gone through whatever bank I had got together and was running around Kings Cross M.A.D. It was like I'd never left. And then to compound things Andrew decided to leave the London after he had an 'awakening' in the form of a vegetarian meal. He decided it was now his destiny to master the nether regions of veganism. And the worst of it was that everyone thought I'd make a great new head chef. Andrew was keen to move quickly so he thought I'd do just fine too, and before I could find a good enough reason to say no, I was back in control of a busy kitchen. I had a serious habit again and a very confusing love life, given my relationships with several other wait-resses were all ongoing while I maintained a drug-fuelled and hateful, junkie-blaming scene with Caroline.

Caroline had a brother with whom she played in a band. And he loved her very much and seemed constantly worried about her. When he sniffed out I was seeing her at least a couple of nights a week, he decided that it was my fault she had decided to use again. He refused to believe that it was actually her personal flaws that saw me using again; he was just looking for someone to blame when she didn't turn up to band practice. The thing was, despite Caroline's fresh appearance and knowing smile, she was an alien-fucking, psycho-candy smack fiend who set an absolutely cracking pace. Pretty soon, despite my increase in pay as head chef, I was broke ten minutes after payday and took to doing some scams that neither of us should ever talk about again. How things could go from relatively smooth and organised to utter fucking chaos was a mystery to me. It was like I had turned into some sort of lightning rod for bad shit happening.

At the time I was self-destructing, again, the early nineties recession hit. Businesses all over Balmain started throwing 'gone broke' parties and closing the doors. Lunches began to slow and the owners of the hotel were increasingly looking to value-add in order to keep the customers they had. As such, I was working harder and longer the quieter the joint got. And the food was good. Everyone was happy with the direction of the menu which, frankly, wasn't that different from what Andrew had been doing. I brought in some twists and turns and pushed the New British thing a little further through the pastry section and with the *amuse bouche*. We were baking bread, taking apart whole fish, using off-cuts of meat and rolling pastry. Wherever we could save a buck we did, and whatever we could do to keep things moving and turning over we did.

On the day I walked past Darling Street Café and saw it closed, two other restaurants in Balmain also closed. It was distressing. Hospitality is one of the first industries hit when the economy slows down and this recession was proving to be no different. Every day, chefs would phone the London looking for work, and we didn't have enough to keep the chefs we had.

As the end of the year approached the owners of the hotel became increasingly keen to infuse the place with a little festive cheer and goodwill, which meant everyone in the kitchen working even harder, doing courtesy bar snacks and more elaborate canapés and a longer list of petits fours that were given away to just about everyone who walked into the joint.

I'd taken on a couple of flatmates in order to ease the rent burden of the house in Annadale. They were both complete and utter drunken stoners. Every night would end in such an elaborate display of empties—empty bottles, bongs, ashtrays, fits and foils—that the used containers would become a work of art, a landscape of the impossible. And it was impossible in the sense that it wasn't possible that so few people could consume so much alcohol and so many drugs and keep their shit together. You could smell the end and this time . . . well, I was just glad I'd taken on a couple of hostages.

New Year's Eve is a date I don't forget any more, infused as it is with the end of things.

After working flat-out for weeks in the lead-up to Christmas and New Year's Eve, Caroline and I decided it was time for a celebration. We agreed to meet up at a club in Kings Cross after work. Given that I could get out of the kitchen sooner than she could finish on the floor, we agreed that I would go score and then we'd hook up. The problem was, there was no dope. Kings Cross was dry, and to say the atmosphere was fraught would be to do an injustice to the palpable sense of murderous rage and blackness that undercut everything else on the neon strip that night. The night-trippers and westies doing their drive-bys weren't aware of how things really were, but to the regulars this was a brave new world. No one could adequately explain what had caused the drought and everyone was blaming everything from the Thai police to Sydney's wharfies to the undercover cops and communism. It had to be a grand conspiracy. There were faces on the street that night that would usually never venture forth, leaving, as they did, the day-to-day running of their business to the working girls and other minions who also took the rap when things turned to shit. But it was like everyone had to check out this bizarre, drugless landscape, in order to see what the strip looked like without the bluster of a ton of smack being exchanged, shot up, and generally moved from A to B.

I don't know why I survived to tell the tale of that particular countdown to midnight fifteen years ago. The doctors said I shouldn't have, but at the time the everyday madness of things seemed so normal. And I still regret not taking the bright yellow envelope that the doctor pushed towards me.

There were a couple of unique things about starting work the morning after an overdose. The first thing was that I got real tired, real early. Primordially, trapped-in-the-swampy-shallows tired. Another thing was that despite my determination never to drink, use drugs or smoke again, I had failed at each ambition by the end of lunch service. And because New Year's Day finds everyone else hungover, there's not a whole lot of the sympathy or understanding that the nearly dead feel is owed to them.

Caroline was upset that I'd stood her up. She wasn't open to the idea of politely sidestepping that reality; she really wanted to talk about it. I was fortunate in that she didn't start work until dinner service and I had a couple of hours' sleep in one of the empty hotel rooms upstairs before I got to tell her why I hadn't showed at the club. It was the hope that I'd hand over the drugs she'd paid me for the day before that meant she stayed long enough to listen to my story of chewing gum and footpaths, ambulance lights and emergency wards. And while she was pleased I hadn't used her deal, she was antsy in a way only a junkie having hung out for nearly twenty-four hours can be.

My job as head chef at the London was becoming more tenuous by the day. My sous-chef had left a few weeks ago, and when I employed Stuart to replace him I knew it wouldn't be long before Stuart replaced me. Stuart had been around the block longer than I had and was a nice guy to boot. He could read the signs at the interview: settle in as sous-chef for a few weeks and then, when this stoner blows it, take over as head chef. What was nice about Stu was that he was in no particular rush to be the king. He didn't mind being sous-chef; he even seemed to like it. But when the other chefs on the line started showing him more respect than me . . . well, I wasn't one to go down without a fight, so I cut his shifts.

There are few things in life more fucked than living in a house as the essential services get cut. The phone is always the first to go, followed by the electricity, and then the gas. After it has happened a few times in various houses you think you'll be prepared for it next time; like, *yeah, yeah, whatever.* But when it began happening in the house in Annandale, it wasn't like that. It was really disappointing.

When the owners of the London sat me down for the inevitable chat, they at least had the grace to do so with a reasonably fat envelope waiting on the table. They seemed genuinely concerned for me. There's a weird thing that happens when you're a young junkie that is impossible to understand until you're a slightly older junkie. You think you're invisible; that your using is some great secret, and if the rest of the world ever found out they would be utterly shocked. But Mathilde—the brassy French dame who owned the London with her husband Bill—crashed through that youthful fantasy with her usual élan.

'You're a junkie,' she said.

'No!' I responded, shocked.

'Yes, you are,' she insisted in her thick French accent.

'I—I'm just . . .' I couldn't quite say what I was.

'You're just a junkie,' she said. 'What did you think? We didn't know? It's a pity, too, because we like you. We think you're a good chef but not now. Now it's too late. You go too far!'

And this scene with Bill and Mathilde was the most no-bullshit scene I'd had in a long time. As such, I felt compelled to defend myself, to explain that I wasn't really a junkie but actually a really good chef who was keen to get over some personal problems. I was actually disgusted with myself when I found it impossible to stop my weak and wilful eyes glancing at the envelope.

'It's all there,' said Bill.

'That's all you care about? Money for your next shot?' Mathilde demanded.

'Is Stuart taking over?' I asked.

'Of course,' Mathilde replied. 'He's a good chef. He likes you but he can't stand to see what you're doing to yourself.'

'I'm just having a bit of a rough trot . . .'

'Oh, please!' Mathilde rolled her eyes.

Despite my youthful, disaffected, drug-induced haze, it was difficult not to get the impression that they'd known for some time about my evil ways. Difficult not to believe that everyone I worked with actually knew me better than I knew myself.

'I hope you manage to get some help, Jimmy,' Bill said.

That was enough for me. I reached for the envelope and got up out of the chair.

'I'll just get my knives.'

And that line, it was like I'd said it a million times now: like getting my knives was what I did rather than use them to any great effect. I didn't have much capacity for shame left, so seeing the other boys didn't bother me. I knew they didn't hate me as a person; they just wanted to get on with the business of cooking a decent menu without some stoner shooting up in the storeroom for morning tea.

And speaking of morning tea . . . I figured I could be out the door and up to the Cross in about seven minutes, which at the time brought a small but discernible spring to my step. I should have been remorseful, mortified and worried about the future, but I wasn't. I was unexpectedly rich, free and feeling wild.

25

Soda, Choc and I sit inside the circular Moroccan hut out by the pool at the back of Rae's. All that remains of our steak and mushroom lunch are the dirty plates.

Alice sends a text message that reads, *I'm worried*.

Soda has pulled out a very cold can of Red Bull for each of us from his secret stash. It's a stash I've looked for in the past and been unable to locate. Now I'm just grateful he has one.

I text Alice back: *I'm way ahead of you this year*.

'That was good, Chef,' Choc says.

'Yeah, fucking awesome, Chef,' Soda seconds.

'Nice piece of beef,' I agree. 'What's the time, Soda?'

'Ten to four, Chef,' Soda replies.

'Okay, here's how it's going to play out this afternoon . . . When Jesse gets back in ten minutes,' I say, as if the thought of Jesse arriving back to work late hadn't crossed my mind, 'I want you to help him box his section for half an hour, Soda.'

'Yes, Chef.'

'I'll get started over on our side. My section isn't too bad. I've got to portion some steaks—those fucking things are selling like hot cakes.' I look at our dirty plates. 'And I've got to cook off a green curry.'

'Yes, Chef.'

I pause as another text from Alice comes through: *Have you left?* I type out a quick reply: *No, but check out the job in the paper . . . in town.*

I turn back to the boys. 'At four thirty, slide back over to woks and just nail it. I really don't think it's too bad but I know you have to clean some more soft-shell crabs, prep some squid and marinate some more whole fish. I'll do a list with you after you pull your section apart.'

'Okay, Chef,' Soda says.

And I'm secretly stoked that I've been able to read the signs about when it's time to leave before Alice had to lay everything out for me. Maybe this is the year I've finally come of age.

And then Jesse wanders in through the back gate.

'Well, here he is, ladies and gentlemen, Jesse fucking James,' I say, trying to conceal my delight that Jesse has returned.

'Sorry about today, Chef. I've just got a bit going on for me with the move and everything,' Jesse says.

'That's okay, Jesse. How did you go with that room?' I ask.

'Yeah, no worries,' he replies. 'All sorted.' And then, rather than stop and chat for a minute with the rest of the crew—like everyone expects him to—Jesse strolls off towards the kitchen.

'You getting something to eat?' I call after him.

'No time, Chef,' Jesse replies. 'I've got to get larder prepped up.'

'Well, boys,' I say to Soda and Choc. 'The team's back on.'

'See you in there, Chef,' Soda says as he gathers up the dirty plates.

'I'm going to phone a kitchen hand!' I call after Soda and Choc.

'Righto, Chef,' Choc calls back. Soda has already disappeared up the tunnel that leads to the kitchen, chasing news from Jesse. Soda will want to smooth things over with his friend, reassure him that the respect is still there, that the fight they had after service is forgotten. And because of the status Jesse has with the boys, Choc and Soda will hang off his every word and study his every move to make sure that order has returned to their world.

I sit inside the Moroccan hut for longer than I should. Relief anchors me to the seat. Alice sends through another text: *I'm scared something is going to break.* And I'm amazed that she's not reading the signs. She would have checked out the ad in the paper by now and know which job I'm talking about.

I'm out of here in a couple of weeks, babe—tops! I text her back, and hear myself sigh deeply as I slump further into the cool cement folds of the seat. I will miss this place but I'm also relieved about the idea of getting my life back.

Please be careful, she writes.

And I've always trusted Alice's emotional radar; she taught me everything I know about what it means to feel . . . but it's worrying me that she's saying this now, because last time we broached the subject of me leaving Rae's, I was insisting on a few more months; get through the high season, see out summer and wave the kids back to school. And now, just when I tell her I'm leaving in a week or two, she starts peaking out.

Be CAREFUL, she repeats, then, *I love you!*

And now I'm really worried, because these are all the usual signs that mean I should grab my knives and head out the gate, asking questions later.

I'm serious about leaving next week, I write. *Day off tomorrow, let's talk then.*

Okay, see you tonight, comes the response.

And I figure she's just bringing me down before I get home. She hates it when it takes me a whole day to unwind enough to play with the kids or discuss things with her. And I hate it too, but my body . . . my body knows who's boss. It's looking forward to a couple of long weeks lulling about some cool ocean shallows. Nothing too vigorous, just sand and sun and water and fun.

But right now, I need to prepare for service tonight. And what that entails is not just a lot of knife work and pare cooking and sauce preparation, it's also an energy thing. For the guests who are dining here this evening, the prospect of dinner at Rae's is something they've been looking forward to. They may have organised a sitter for the kids or booked a table six months ago or even saved up for the experience. Dinner at Rae's is not inexpensive, particularly if you like to drink wine or champagne. And ninety-five percent of our clientele know that— they expect to pay at least a couple of hundred dollars per head—but for one couple out in the restaurant tonight, this meal is going to be a once-in-a-year event, something they've saved money for and dreamt about. It's the pressure of that, of all the various expectations and swirling desires and moments of anticipated pleasure that function as a motivating force, which compels me out of my comfortable seat and into the office to organise a kitchen hand.

Carla agrees to operate as our dishwasher tonight because she wants a start in the kitchen as a chef. In previous careers, Carla has worked as a television actress, a lingerie model and a waitress. Carla's not your usual kitchen job applicant in that she's platinum blonde, early thirties and turning heads is still her primary occupation. Initially I was deeply sceptical about Carla and it took some prodding from Vinnie before I agreed that she could try out as a kitchen hand. I even agreed that if she was still turning up to work in the galley after a few months I might consider training her as a mature-age apprentice chef.

My reticence about taking on Carla is founded on twenty-something years of experience in a whole lot of different kitchens. It's experience that tells me people generally start out in kitchens when they're young, then move on to other careers as they get a little older, rather than the other way around. And they do this because the life of a chef, particularly an apprentice chef or a chef lower down the kitchen hierarchy, is physically demanding and often thankless. Carla never did strike me as someone who was going to cope with such a reality. To my surprise, though, she took on the role of kitchen hand with dedication and enthusiasm. She never stopped telling me or anyone else who'd listen she was only doing it to get a start as a chef, but nonetheless she impressed with her attention to detail and a capacity to say yes to starting work at ridiculously short notice. Whenever someone does that enough times, which is to say they take one for the team by agreeing to spend their night cleaning the kitchen, the possibility of something radical—like a little respect from the other chefs—becomes a possibility.

When I phoned her to ask her to come in tonight, she said she would but that I needed to start thinking about a position on the line for her, something regular. It wasn't a threat, it's just the way it is; if a person gets some skills in the kitchen they realise that if things turn to shit or they get sick of a place they can move on and employ those skills somewhere else. And while she wasn't able to do Jesse's job if he walked out or didn't turn up to work one day—or suddenly got sacked—the other boys were more than capable of sliding up the line so that Carla could start down on pastry and help out in larder. Such a job description was a full-time position and she was more than keen.

'Hey, Chefs,' Carla greets everyone as she enters the kitchen, grabbing a piece of fresh picked crab that Jesse is working on in the larder section.

'You want some sauce with that?' Jesse asks her.

'You keep it, Chef,' she replies. 'Wouldn't want you to run out.'

'How much weight have you put on since you started here, Carla?' Jesse continues, feigning concern.

'Well, let's see. Over the last three months while I've been covering your arse, I've probably put on about three kilos, Jesse.'

'Three!' Jesse laughs. 'What comes after ten, Carla?'

'You sweetheart.' Carla grins and then ramps up the dishwasher so that any reply is drowned out. She cups her hand over her ear and looks at Jesse, who is saying something in response, but shakes her head to let him know she can't hear him.

Like I said, the boys will learn. Carla's been around some different city blocks to these boys, even if they've been in a whole lot more kitchens. As a rule I don't attempt to shut down the piss-taking and the banter too early because I find that if a head chef does that, tensions come out sideways and in between things: people start forging weird allegiances and cliques that exclude some and elevate others. Fuck that; let some of the heat and tension which builds between any group of people dissipate during service and the team is all the better for it.

'One hour until service, people!' I call out.

'Yes, Chef,' they reply.

'Choc, how's pastry section looking?'

'Fucked, Chef,' replies Choc. 'We need a new coconut cake and vanilla ice cream and . . . everything else.'

'I liked you better when you didn't swear, Choc. Please, mate, for the children, keep it clean.'

'Yes, Chef.' Choc is pissed off that he's been left to pick up the mess that the pastry section always is.

'Carla,' I yell down to the galley, 'give Choc a hand for an hour before service.'

'I've got a lot of dishes to get through here, Chef,' she replies.

'Two words, Carla,' I call back to her.

'Yes, Chef,' she yells back, like, *what would I know?* And that's just who Carla is. She overcompensates in all her communication because she's thirty-something and just starting out in the kitchen. And it's probably got something to do with the fact she looks like Marilyn Monroe and isn't married to some banker. Most fairytales would cast Carla as a guest of the hotel rather than our kitchen hand tonight. But that's not my problem.

'You need a tissue, love?' Jesse asks Carla.

'Fuck off, Jesse,' says Carla.

'Chef,' Jesse calls over to me, 'Carla's being mean to me.'

'Listen up, people,' I warn everyone. 'During service tonight I don't want to hear any voices other than mine, okay?'

'Yes, Chef,' they chorus.

'You're the voice . . .' Scotty calls into the kitchen as he dumps off the empty platter and plates from Vinnie's table.

'Try and understand it,' I say, finishing the line that I'm fond of saying.

'Vinnie's leaving before the bill hits the table. I think his new friends might get a nasty little surprise there.' Scotty laughs.

'I thought he was buying them lunch?' I say.

'I think they did too.'

'They coming back for dinner?' I ask him.

'No chance,' Scotty says. 'Elle's in town, apparently, and they want to go somewhere decent for dinner.' Which is a joke that Vinnie likes to serve cold to the chefs at

Rae's when he chooses to entertain visiting celebrities at one of the other fine-dining restaurants in town.

'Are you tagging along, Scotty?' I ask.

'I might go down for a beer after work,' says Scotty in a very noncommittal tone.

'Really, mate, I didn't think Elle was your type.'

'Paris will probably be there,' Scotty adds with all the nonchalance he can muster.

'Yeah, and she might need a butler,' chimes in Jesse.

'Fuck off, Jesse,' Scotty replies. 'If I want your opinion I'll ask a chef.'

'Oh, that hurts.' Jesse points his knife into his chest. 'Really, Scotty, that gets right in there.' And Jesse appears to actually dig his knife hard into his chest, coughing a couple of times from his efforts.

'Go easy, Jesse,' I suggest.

'You're such a fuckwit, Jesse,' Carla adds. 'If everyone's going to the Beachie after work, I'll come down with you, Scotty.'

As far as Scotty's fantasies go in regards to impossible dates with beautiful women, this is as close to scoring a bullseye as he's thrown in a while.

'You're such a slut, Carla,' Jesse says in a high-pitched squeal.

'Oh, that's so sweet! That's what your daddy said,' Carla fires back.

'Back to work, people. I don't give a fuck what you do after service tonight but right now I want you to focus on your sections and make sure they are completely fucking set. If anyone runs out of anything, I am going to take it personally. Does everyone understand?' I yell louder than is necessary because I want to call their attention to the tasks at hand.

'Yes, Chef!'

Scotty takes his cue and disappears out of the kitchen.

'Soda, get over here on woks now. Jesse, are you all right over there?' I ask.

'Yes, Chef,' replies Jesse. 'Can I go back on my section tomorrow, Chef?'

'See, here's the thing, Jesse. You and I, my friend, have a day off tomorrow and these scumbags don't. And tomorrow,' I remind him, 'is just a day away.'

'Yes!' Jesse sounds ecstatic. 'I almost forgot.'

'Well, get cracking, mate. Carla, are you on larder tomorrow?' I ask.

'Probably,' she replies. 'I'll be anywhere Joseph puts me.'

'That'll be on your knees,' replies Jesse.

'You're sounding more like your daddy every day, sweetheart,' Carla says. 'Is he out of jail yet?'

And as a tactic, Carla's use of Jesse's father as a comeback is both clever and dangerous. No one knows too much about Jesse's father, including Jesse, and for Carla to be going there . . . well, it's opening a door into the unknown. And Jesse is starting to tense up.

'Jesse,' I suggest, 'go have a cigarette before service. Which means a four-minute break. Everyone can go for a quick smoke before dinner, one at a time, okay?'

'Yes, Chef,' everyone calls back, except Jesse, who has already gone.

'Carla,' I say, 'go easy, for chrissake.'

'He'll learn,' she says.

'He's got a bit going on at the moment, Carla,' adds Soda.

'He's a big boy, darling,' Carla coos across the kitchen to Soda.

Carla and Soda are like a special club of two, each of them born with something special that most folks don't get. The thing that divides them, though, is that Carla's good looks, wit and charm are about fifteen years more used up than Soda's—and Soda knows enough about life to know he doesn't want to end up where she is now.

'Why do you always stick up for him anyway, Soda?' asks Carla, with her serious face on.

'I don't know.' Soda shrugs. 'We're on the line together.'

'That doesn't mean he's always right about things,' she says.

'I know that,' Soda says, getting irritated. 'It's just the way it is. He sticks up for me and I stick up for him.'

'He wouldn't stick up for you like you do for him,' Carla persists.

'Just do the dishes, Carla,' Soda says, cool as ice. 'I don't want to talk about Jesse or me or anything else. Just do your job and keep your trap shut.'

And it's not as if Carla hasn't heard it all before. Soda's the only person in the kitchen who can talk to her like that. They've got each other figured out and I don't interrupt them. The thing about Carla is that she's a talker, and what she talks about is the same thing a lot of women like to talk about, which is people. And relationships. And it confuses the hell out of the boys, who would rather not talk at all than discuss that stuff. For a moment Carla doesn't say anything. Which makes everyone happy. And in the silence, we all catch a fleeting glimpse of how stressed out we are, and how much further we've got to go in order to get through the rest of this crazy high season.

26

No one, least of all me, has ever accused my mother of being overly maternal, but when she phoned me a few days into the shiny New Year, which began with an overdose, I was touched. Indeed, I was in a space that might generally be thought of as very forgiving. After getting sacked from the London Hotel and turning my fat severance envelope into a scrawled list of crazy things to do, I was open to the idea that people could change—that people should change, regularly, mix things up. And they should do this because no one wants to stagnate in life; change is positive, it's progressive. My greatest problem was that I'd tried a lot of different avenues in order to facilitate meaningful change and each such avenue had ended in a cul-de-sac of crap.

My mother had decided to do the country New South Wales brothel tour, which was apparently quite lucrative. A tour of duty like that saw a bunch of girls leave Sydney in a rental car or minivan and basically rip things up around various country towns. Someone obviously does all the organising with the local brothels and the word gets passed around the community grapevine and before a struggling young chef can say, 'How about a small loan, Mum?' the girls pack up and move on to the next digs.

The thing is, mid-tour, my mother had been rescued—again—by a small-town Prince Charming who owned the local drive-through liquor store. And he had taken to parading her around the streets like a prized possession and had even made some commitments to give up drinking. In fact, what became apparent talking to my mother was that she was now a New Age freak who was determined to change her life and resolve her past. It sounded to me like she might be amenable to the idea that she owed me something. I figured anyway you looked at it she owed me at least the means to get the fuck out of my desperate situation in Annandale and find alternative accommodation. And because she'd left the rest of the tour party and moved in with Prince Charming, she had a phone number and an address and was open to the idea of a visit. This was good; this was colour and movement, which distracted me from the bleeding obviousness of my own sad demise. So, with a ridiculously optimistic spirit of abandon, I jumped on my unregistered, uninsured and unlicensed motorbike, and drove west into the setting sun.

To have recently survived a massive overdose and still be semi-using and hanging out was an uncomfortable experience; but riding a very large motorbike made it less painful than it was when sitting in a small room with no money, electricity, gas or phone. The open road, nature, working people who functioned outside of commercial kitchens, these were all things that were fascinating in a flying-by kind of fashion. I had no interest in engaging with anyone; in fact, I was suffering regular anxiety attacks. Every time I passed a police car or idled through a small country town, I felt a cold panic crawl up my spine. I also felt strongly that I was heading for an ending of sorts, that I was going to be stopped or arrested, and the greatest problem with that was the lack of options that being locked in a prison cell presented. My arms were so pockmarked from shooting up, my skin so fiercely unhappy with what was going on inside my body, that the chances of me explaining away my lack of licence and registration to some earnest young copper were next to none.

I was desperate to give up the drugs. And it wasn't that I hadn't been desperate during every other attempt to do so, it was just that life always dished the drugs back up to me in such a way that promised things would be different this time. Only it never was. It was only ever more of the same. And worse than that, what was becoming normal was so far removed from broader societal notions of normalcy that I genuinely feared for my mental health. It was like I was looking for a brick wall to end the madness. I was so worn down from working so many hours in too many different kitchens with such a cocktail of drug addictions clanging around my system, that I was open to anything that presented as a solution to getting straight. I was the perfect candidate for the Scientologists, the Hare Krishnas, various born-again freaks or basically anyone or anything that might offer a solution to my particular set of problems. I understood clearly why semi-intelligent people could believe that human beings were descended from aliens. I would have run with any of it if it had got me straight and ended the madness in my head.

A lot of people wonder what drives seemingly good people to such ridiculous levels of self-abandonment with drug addiction. Let me tell you, the thing that becomes impossible to escape from in the end, the thing that prolongs the endgame of collapse, is simply the madness of a million incessant, insistent, highly critical, screaming voices inside your head. And the only way to shut them up is with a shot of smack. In the end, all I was doing was killing the voices. I didn't expect any pleasure or a rush or some cosy stone; those things belonged to more innocent days.

So as I'm ringing out my Suzuki 1100 to two hundred and forty k an hour along the Snowy Mountains Highway, the idea of crashing or even being killed or ending up in a hospital or wrapped around a tree wasn't so much the end of the world as the end of madness: a way to shut my fucking head up about a whole lot of shit that I could no longer stand to listen to. It wasn't like the voices in my drug-fucked mind were delivering new information; it was just madness.

A doctor later explained to me that the functioning brain can be reduced to a serious of chemical reactions, and that what I was doing by using such a cocktail of self-injected chemicals was creating chaos inside my brain. The voices were chemical reactions gone wrong, misfires, random correcting efforts, various inhibitors reacting against various stimulants. But at the time, well, when I finally pulled into the driveway at Mum's, I was a little more open than I might normally have been to the notion of some instantaneous New Age cure-all. So when an exorcism was mentioned as a means to rid me of my drug addiction, it made more sense than it should have.

The idea was that I'd picked up a 'lost soul' during one of my overdoses and it was responsible for my drug addiction. I must admit, the idea that I didn't have to take any personal responsibility for the last ten years of chaos and torment was appealing. You probably had to be there to believe that such a solution could be met with a straight face, let alone enthusiasm, but like they say in the lower courthouses come Monday morning, 'It all made sense at the time, Your Honour.'

A bird's-eye view of Wagga Wagga in summer reveals a town that is flat and hot. It's fucking steaming hot. What moisture there is gets shimmered into a mid-morning haze and by lunch you're ready for an aspirin and a quiet lie down in the broom closet or somewhere else very dark and silent. Frankly, I found the conditions cruel. I'd hung out off smack enough times to lose count but this was something else.

My mother was highly energised; she was on a mission. There was a problem, which was me, and there was a solution, which was a New Age exorcism. I did ask if we might be able stretch the budget to a Catholic priest, but apparently they were out of fashion. By now I felt so bad that I believed the only thing that might possibly 'cure' me or take away the screeching aches and joint pain was a drama big enough to literally scare the fucking creepy-crawlies out of my legs. As such, the actual ceremony whereby the 'lost soul' was exorcised from my sweating, pinpricked carcass was all a bit of a let-down. Where I felt the need for fire and brimstone, the New Age priest brought calm and inner focus. Where I felt the need for screaming, blood, guts and glory, the New Age priest brought an elderly woman whose children probably really loved her. She was scared. She was more scared than me in that motel room in Wagga Wagga. She was out-of-her-fucking-depth scared and when I sensed that—when the penny hit the deck and spun—the sound of the spinning represented some kind of death knell.

The exorcism wouldn't, shouldn't and hadn't worked. After the twenty minutes of quiet mantras and closed-eyed aura waving I hit a new low. And down there, in the deepest valley, where hope has all but gone, one's mind is reduced to symbols and imagery: the lilies of the field; angry dragons; the eternal prisoner. It was like whatever innocence my soul might have held tight in a piggy bank somewhere, cracked open and spilled out over the barren land that represented all my possible futures. And perhaps someone less leavened by a heroin addiction might have seen that as proof that the exorcism was responsible for a surrender of sorts, but I chose to believe it was the utter failure of the exercise that brought about such a strong sense of hopelessness. Why fight it? my spilling spirit sighed. Once a junkie, always a junkie.

After the ceremony, I did my best to avoid disappointing my mother and her team of willing helpers. I didn't want to reject their sincerity or goodwill. All the same, help, that most difficult and nebulous of things—that most easy-to-get-wrong of things—seemed further away than ever.

I reasoned that if my own mother couldn't help me, even though she genuinely wanted to, there was little hope that some random other person might be able to. In fact, it seemed that I was going to have to adjust to the reality of a life of crime. The only problem with that was all the romance of such a proposition had been so thoroughly wrung from all my previous efforts that prison was starting to look like not so much a dead-end as the best of all possible outcomes. And yet . . .

The idea of being a late-twenties sex toy for men twice my size provided sufficient motivation for me to carry on looking for alternative cures. What I didn't realise at the time was that all my information about what it *meant* to be a junkie was information that had come from other junkies and irregular snippets from an impossibly biased and uninformed media. While it may seem absurd now, I didn't know about detoxes or rehabs; I didn't know about NA meetings or controlled-using programs; and while I had mates on methadone, their general demeanour and sense of wellbeing was not what I was looking for. And I didn't want to be Straight-backed Sally, either. Really, I didn't know what I wanted outside of recognising a need to quit using smack.

Mum and her New Age priest friend created a blue aura around me for the five-hour motorbike ride back to Sydney. And as I sat on the resprayed, matt-black Suzuki 1100 with my helmet pulled down tight, my bony body wrapped in a Stagg leather jacket and Levis 501s, the engine all throaty beneath me, I smiled as I realised I'd be back in Sydney tonight. I knew that it was the end of something. I didn't know what my next move would be or which town, city or country I would end up in, but I knew it was time to leave the house in Annandale and put some distance between me and Balmain which, as a suburb, was becoming altogether too small and judgemental.

The idea of being back in Sydney brought with it the realisation that I could get on again before I began sorting out things to do with work and accommodation. I figured I could be out of Sydney in about three or four days and I may as well keep things as simple as possible and continue using until I was some place else. And while that might appear a self-defeating approach to things after my efforts to get off smack, it was actually quite logical. To completely remove the smack from my system as I attempted to bring about some lasting changes would be like sending a starving person to the gym. On some deep level I had surrendered to the idea that 'my way' wasn't working. And while I didn't yet have any idea about what a better way might look like, life was compelling me on, somewhere. And it was fucking painful. As such, the idea of popping a vein and pushing a shot of smack home saw me tearing up the stretch of country between Wagga Wagga and Sydney in record time.

The obstacles that stand between a junkie and his obsession are really no obstacles at all. I flew through towns at a hundred and forty k an hour; I overtook buses on narrow stretches of winding road, slumped down over the petrol tank, the engine screaming, hungry for oil. I flew past police cars travelling in the opposite direction that flashed their brake lights before realising the race was over. They couldn't catch me and they knew it. Maybe I'd crash, maybe I'd die, but if I didn't, I was racing straight to the Golden Mile.

As I pushed the motorbike through the outskirts of Sydney and pulled onto Parramatta Road, lights were coming on in buildings as the sun went down on another day. The bike was not happy, coughing and wheezing as I zigzagged between cars on my way up to the Cross. I didn't think about work or home or Mum or friends; my body was seizing up, knees locked, wrists frozen from four hours on the highway. Dusk is the saddest part of the day when life is getting you down. If hope springs eternal, it's a morning thing. Come sunset, it's obvious that any optimism that may have risen with the morning is now so used up it's not just meaningless, but painfully so.

But such pain is also comforting when you find a crowd to share the burden with. And up at the Cross, with its massive Coca-Cola sign flicking across the night sky, a madcap collection of optimists down on their luck shared the stage. As soon as I revved up Victoria Road I felt better than I had in weeks. I'd borrowed a few hundred from my mother and was confident I could be styling in no time flat. I parked the bike, slotted the helmet and headed up to see the girls.

It's rare, but sometimes everything goes right for a junkie looking to get on. I've seen it happen for others and shaken my head and wondered how they did it. Most times I just put it down to the last dregs of charm. But when I spotted an old friend from the Bondi days and he hooked me up with the shiniest of the local crew and I got to put my shot away in a nicely tiled bathroom in one of the better restaurants on the main drag, the relief was such that I cried. It wasn't the sadness of using again or of being a hopeless junkie; they were tears for the end of pain. And when I joined my friend in the restaurant, I spotted a chef I knew working in the open kitchen who insisted on cooking dinner for me and my old mate Paul. And who was I to argue? I knew things couldn't last, but tonight I was back and I was grateful.

It was a mistake to let the motorbike cool down. After dinner and scoring some takeaway smack, I slid back onto the bike, turned the key and pushed the electric ignition. Nothing. And it wasn't just nothing, it was super-sized nothing. I tried the kick-start but that made such a sick gurgling noise that I knew my run of good fortune had just ended. I didn't fight it; I was fully Buddha about such things now that I was comfortably off-chops. So I headed up to the taxi rank and caught a ride home to Annandale.

Walking into a house where the essential services have been cut for a couple of weeks is weird. It's like it smells of people, but no one lives there any more. When my two flatmates appeared, they weren't actually too concerned about the no-electricity thing. In fact, they'd adapted to their off-the-grid existence by constructing an elaborate fire-in-a-drum situation in the back garden. The resilience was touching, inspirational even, but the smell . . . Where the boys wouldn't go was the cold shower.

They seemed pleased to have me back, at least until I started talking about how it was probably time to move on and go our separate ways. It was then that they started to talk about what could be done to heat cold water, how they might be able to construct a boiler system with elaborate pulleys and strings . . .

'Boys,' I said, 'we haven't paid the rent in over a month. How long do you reckon they're going to let us stay?'

'Fair enough,' said Dave. 'I might crash with my mate over in Balmain.'

'Is he looking for flatmates, is he?' asked Benny, his voice hopeful.

'No, mate, he's not,' replied Dave.

'But he's a mate?' enquired Benny.

'He's my mate, mate,' said Dave.

'Yeah, but we're all mates, Dave,' said Benny.

'Fellas,' I said, 'we've got twenty-four hours and we're out the door. All right?'

They nodded, accepting the inevitable.

'How's the bike going, Jimmy?' said Benny.

'Yeah, not good, mate,' I replied. 'It's still up the Cross. I think I've blown the conrod.'

'But you're not sure,' said Benny, ever hopeful.

'Yeah, no, I am sure, mate. The conrod's come out the side of the casing.'

'Oh, that's fucked then,' confirmed Dave, who was an expert in all things mechanical.

We sat silent in the darkness for a while. There wasn't a lot of huffing and puffing about future plans or wonderful tomorrows. We all knew we'd landed on our knees rather than our feet and there seemed little point in going over old ground.

'Is Flick's car still down the laneway?' I asked the boys.

'Oh yeah, but it's fucked, mate,' said Benny.

'It's got no rego, no back seat, and the lights don't work,' Dave explained.

'Does it go?' I persisted.

'Yeah, it goes. We started it up the other night to listen to the races. But you wouldn't get out of the laneway before the cops were all over you, mate.'

'Yeah, you're probably right, mate,' I agreed, nodding.

'Where're you thinking of going, Jimmy?' asked Benny.

'Thought I might head up to Nimbin.'

'Oh yeah. Sounds like a plan,' said Benny.

'You won't fucking get there in that piece of shit,' said Dave.

'Oh, fucking lighten up, Dave. We're just talking, mate,' I told him.

'Yeah, well, I'm just telling you, the car's a heap of shit and you won't make it out of Annandale.'

'Well, thanks for the tip, mate,' said Benny. He looked at me. 'So we've got an early start then?'

'Yeah,' I said.

27

Last time I'd headed north I'd got busted doing my drug-run-gone-wrong to Brisbane. It wasn't a pleasant memory. Now, sitting behind the wheel of the heap-of-shit Corolla, which really was a transport of last resort, it was difficult not to imagine this current expedition ending badly as well. Still, Benny and I remained quite cheery. We'd managed to get on to some particularly low-grade, teeth-grinding smack as well as a few foils of Rohypnol. As the hours of driving wore on, however, the pressure of waiting for the axe to fall began to take its toll. We started fighting over radio stations and petrol costs, and whether or not I was speeding (which was something we couldn't accurately determine because the speedometer was broken). Very little actually worked on the old two-door Corolla. It was quite amazing that the engine ran as well as it did and that the wheels and gearbox continued to do their thing.

Our biggest problem was that we stood out. Because Benny and I weren't planning to go back to Sydney, we'd stuffed everything we owned into and onto the car. There was shit strapped to the roof, the boot wouldn't fully close and had to be bungy-strapped shut; the back seat was piled so high with garbage bags and boxes of crap that I couldn't see out the back window through the rear-view mirror.

It's strange how at certain times when I've really needed to be invisible, things have transpired to make me a fucking rock star. People would overtake us and stare out their window, half laughing, half shaking their heads. And because the lights didn't work on the old Corolla, we had to take the daylight option. Petrol stations were the worst of it. People just openly laughed when they saw us drive in and stop. And I guess it was something of a sight, a couple of junkies down on their luck, out for a . . . long Sunday drive.

Driving into a random breath testing station at two o'clock on a balmy mid-autumn afternoon in Armidale wasn't quite the blaze of glory we'd hoped for. As the cops waved us over into their cunningly hidden testing area, it was a relief in many ways.

Benny and I looked at each other and laughed.

'Well, mate, this is it then,' I said.

'Looks like it.'

'I reckon top speed is probably about a hundred in this old girl,' I said.

'It'd be good for a laugh, though,' said Benny, his eyes glinting at the thought of a *Funniest Home Videos*-type car-chase scene.

But I glided to a stop. I figured that the police would have to take some responsibility for us now. We were obviously not only fucked up, but absolute gangsters.

The officer leant in the window. 'Driver's licence?'

'Don't have one,' I replied.

'Rego?' a second copper asked.

'Don't think so. It's not my car.'

'Stolen, is it?' he asked.

'Nah. Not really.'

'He said it's not really stolen, Terry,' the young copper said to the older cop, feigning goodwill.

'Yeah, well, that should be sweet then,' the older copper responded. 'You handy with a screwdriver are you, son?'

'Yeah, not bad,' I said.

Glancing across at Benny, I smiled. We were up for this shit. Give us your worst. We'd probably be behind bars in half an hour enjoying a mug of sweet tea and some Vegemite toast.

'Well, get out of the car and take the plates off then,' the older cop said.

'Yeah, no worries,' I agreed, not wanting to aggravate the situation by spinning a yarn, which was something I'd have done in the past.

This time felt different. Benny and I were both completely over it. We were hanging out badly even with the low-grade skank we were on. And ever since my trip to Wagga Wagga, a strong sense that life was going to change had stayed with me. If this was to be the event that brought about that change, so be it.

As I took the number plates off the car, the older

cop was busy writing a whole lot of shit down while his offsider was in the police car phoning home. When I handed the officer the number plates, he handed me three tickets and said, 'Have a nice day.'

I was stunned. Were these cunts blind? And not only blind but fucking stupid? We were drug-fucked gangsters, for chrissake, ripping up the highway in a stolen car. The tickets for unlicensed, unregistered and uninsured driving totalled into a very nasty figure that only added to the surreal nature of what had just gone down.

'Jesus,' said Benny. 'We're free.'

'Well, fuck me sideways,' I said. 'I really can't believe it.'

Benny shook his head in wonder. 'What the fuck are we going to do now?'

That was the question I didn't want to hear because I was sick to fucking death of pondering such matters. 'I don't fucking know, mate. Why don't you put your thinking cap on and jot a few ideas down.'

'Oi, steady on, mate,' Benny protested.

'Well, I don't fucking know what we'll do, all right? I've fucking had it with figuring out what to do.'

'Yeah, I was just saying, mate . . .' Benny was starting to sulk.

'I know what you were saying. And the answer is I don't know. We've got fuck-all money, fuck-all drugs and we're a long way from Nimbin.'

'Well, what's up in Nimbin anyway?' said Benny, looking around the parklands of Armidale.

'Oh yeah, right. You think we should set up camp here in sunny fucking Armidale, do you? That's your input, is it? Benny to the rescue . . . switch on the sirens, sound the alarm, here comes fucking Fireman Sam.'

'Nah, I wasn't saying that.'

'Mate,' I said, 'what's in Nimbin is freaks like us. All right? We'll be among our own. It's not quite Hollywood but there's weed growing down the main street and people who don't give a fuck if you stop to roll some of it up. You think we'd bump into those sorts of people here?'

'No, mate. I was just saying—'

'Yeah, well, I know what you were saying.'

'Well, I've still got a few hundred, Jimmy,' Benny volunteered.

'Righto then,' I said. 'Let's idle the car down to that motel and make camp.'

'You think we should drive?'

'Mate!' I said, exasperated. 'A bloke can't get arrested in this town.'

'Yeah, I guess,' said Benny, getting more comfortable with the idea of being a free man.

'C'mon. Get in. We'll just roll down the hill, mate.'

'Nah, mate, I think I'll just walk down and meet you there.'

'Oh, right. That's how it is, is it?'

'Nah, it's not how it is . . . I was just saying.'

'No fucking worries,' I said, angry now, revving the shit out of the Corolla and setting off a particularly toxic chain reaction through the exhaust system. Then I clunked the car into gear and did a very piss-weak bunny-hop and sped down the road to the motel.

★★★

212

Once we'd settled into the Settler's Inn at Armidale, things started to feel a little better. Benny and I weren't really speaking to each other but at least we were civil and glad for the comfortable beds and clean sheets. The old couple at reception were very pleasant, which was the greatest surprise of my recent life. It had become rare for people I didn't know to be remotely kind to me or even stop to give me the time of day. In retrospect, they were probably more scared than anything; not that I felt like a dangerous person or was anything other than polite. It was probably the palpable sense of desperation we gave off that frightened people.

All I needed from these kind, elderly motel managers was a place to sleep; a room to lock the rest of the world out of while I put on the television and dreamt of a time when I hadn't had my particular set of problems. It was a dream that seemed to roll back a long time. I'd been 'up' for so long by then, ferreting out a living, crashing and burning, talking it up and pushing the needle in, that I was tired in a way that a young man should never be. There was not a single thing I felt I could be grateful for; everything felt too heavy a burden and too hard to hold. And the worst of it was the strong sense I had that as far as the rest of the world was concerned, I had brought it all on myself, because in a very real way I knew I had. Sure, there'd been extenuating circumstances, and there were people to blame and even some good reasons to justify a bit of carry-on . . . but at the end of the day it was my life and I'd run out of answers.

It wasn't as if I'd planned any of this; it felt like I hadn't taken a breath since I'd left high school as a

fifteen-year-old kid, and through circumstances unfold-
ing had ended up here in this motel. What scared me
most about that was the idea that I might suddenly stop;
might become catatonic beneath my polyester quilt in the
floral surrounds of Armidale. I fantasised that I could just
lock myself in the room and see how the rest of the world
dealt with the problem. And yet there was a crazy part
of my brain, the mad scientist, the eternal optimist, that
kept at me, pushing me towards the 'answer'. It was like,
if I could just join all the pieces of the puzzle together,
then the whole thing might somehow lock together in
such a way that would not just make sense of how I was
feeling but shine a fucking light on things.

Let me give you a bird's-eye view of Armidale in mid-
autumn. Come evening time, it's a very pretty little
country town. The township itself is nestled in a valley
where fog sets in most nights. When it gets cold, smoke
trails out of the many chimneys that line the roofs of
the village houses. And there's a very pleasant-looking
historic bluestone university on the edge of town. The
whole feel is quaint; it's the sort of place that a lot of
people might stop at and wonder what it would be like
to live there.

I slipped out of the motel after dark to organise some
food and wine for us. Benny had run the local river dry
with a half-hour steaming hot shower and then crashed
out on the queen-size bed.

As I wandered around the streets of Armidale trying
to decide on Chinese or fried chicken, I stopped off at a

phone box and—in utter desperation—opened the phone-book and dropped my finger onto a random number. I rang the number and, as I listened to it ring, wondered what I was going to say to whoever answered. My finger had landed on some business called Triple 7 something. And it sounded good. It sounded like a code, like there might be something hidden there, and when the guy at the other end of the line answered, 'Triple 7, can I help you?' my immediate response was, 'Yeah.'

And after an extended pause the guy said, 'Okay, what do you need?'

'I don't know,' I said.

'Are you looking for some advertising space? We're an advertising firm.'

'No. No, I'm not looking for advertising space,' I replied.

There was another long pause, during which he seemed to sense this wasn't just a prank call.

'I'm not really sure what I can do,' he said.

'No. Nor am I.' I gently hung up the phone.

It was an intimate call. A weird, softly spoken and utterly random call for help where the caller had no idea what questions to ask and the guy who'd answered had no idea what to say in response. As I placed the receiver back in its cradle, it was hard not to realise how desperate I had become. Pressure will do funny things to a person and everyone is going to deal with things differently, but I was critically aware that I didn't have much sane time left. I was straddling a line, seesawing between madness and something else. And my greatest problem was that I had lost contact with, or even a sense of, what that something else was. I could no longer recall what normal felt like.

I decided on Chinese, a six-pack of beer and a bottle of red, though I didn't even feel like drinking. The powder I'd been shooting up was so riddled with chalk I had to throw away what little I had left. I'd tried burning off whatever they'd cut the pasty skank with by holding a lighter to the bottom of the spoon, but what remained after was no better so I just flushed it. It had been getting harder to breathe the further north we got and I eventually had to acknowledge it was more likely the result of shooting up chalk dust than the side effects of breathing clean country air.

Benny was up when I got back to the motel room. He had the television on and lights going and seemed quite happy propped up among his eight pillows and floral doona.

'Well, hello, Princess,' I said. 'How's that great big bloody bed then?'

The sleep had obviously done Benny good because instead of biting back he just laughed and took the piss.

''Bout fucking time with the dinner, mate. I was about to phone Pizza Hut.'

'We wouldn't want you to strain your finger now, mate, would we? What would we do if that happened?'

'You'd have to pick me nose, for one thing.' He laughed.

'Yeah, and feed it to you, I suppose.'

'Nah, mate, I haven't chewed on me snot since I got off the gack,' Benny said.

'Mate, you'd fucking starve if you stopped eating your snot.'

'What'd you get?'

'Chinese and red wine,' I said, holding up the packages. 'Who the fuck said crime doesn't pay?'

Benny went straight back to sleep after dinner. The combination of food, red wine and a comfortable bed quickly lulled him back to dreamland. Meanwhile, as I sat on my single bed, the television playing soundlessly in the corner, I drew the curtains back and stared out at the old green Corolla. I realised, looking at the car, that it represented a picture of what I had managed to achieve in my twenty-eight years. And it was a picture that, even if you were talented at such things, couldn't be spun into a story where success was even remotely connected to the themes of the narrative.

I'd spoken briefly to Benny about getting up while it was still dark and making a run for Nimbin. It was only about four hours up the road if we didn't plan on implementing the Stop, Revive and Survive plan. After sliding the curtain closed and flicking off the television, I lay in the darkness for a few minutes and resolved that, if I woke up early enough, I'd shake Benny out of his slumber and hit the highway. How bad could it be? We'd get nicked again, probably score a few more tickets, then try to make it all the way to the Promised Land. I was still surprised the police hadn't taken us down to the station or impounded the car or done something that had relieved us, or at least me, of the burden of having to make further decisions.

★★★

Ten o'clock in the morning in Armidale is reasonably busy. It's not Pitt Street but there's plenty happening, including the motel's maid banging on our door and insisting—in the nicest possible broken English—that it was time to arise from our beds and face the day. And what was good about that was that we hit the ground running. Benny headed straight for another pounding hot shower while I placated the maid and told her we'd be out in fifteen minutes.

The car didn't look quite so vulnerable in the morning. Somehow the colour and movement of a busy weekday allowed the faintly ridiculous nature of the Corolla's bulging outline to blend more into the background. I jammed the rest of our shit into the car and strolled down to reception and paid the bill. Once again, the old couple were completely charming; they didn't make a big deal about payment or being late or using half the town's water supply; they just accepted payment graciously, not asking too many questions in the process, and bade us well on our journey. Their graceful hospitality has become something I recall in moments when I'm working in a hotel or a restaurant and a customer strolls in who is obviously not a natural fit with the surroundings. If they're looking for kindness and hospitality, then I try not to make a big fuss and give them what they've come for. And more generally, whether it's in the family home, at a social function or in the context of work, hospitality addresses the human body and its universal needs for food, drink and shelter. That's what we do in hospitality; we don't so much address people as bodies. It doesn't and absolutely shouldn't matter if you're black, white or brindle, rich, middle class or down on your luck—everyone has to meet those basic needs of food, drink and shelter in order to survive. Sometimes I think we get things a little screwed up with grading systems, restaurant scores or numbers of stars, rather than acknowledging our roles as either host or guest with a spirit of hospitableness.

As Benny and I waved our goodbyes to Ma and Pa Hospitality at reception, I turned the smoking four-cylinder beast towards the train station. I'd convinced Benny we should load our collective shit onto a train and then catch a bus to Nimbin. We'd be able to collect our treasured possessions at a later date from the Lismore railway station. It all sounded fair enough to Benny, whose spirits had picked up remarkably as a result of a long night of uninterrupted slumber.

'You're a cheery soul this morning,' I said to him.

'Yeah, not too bad,' he replied.

'Nearly there now,' I said.

'Yeah,' replied Benny, with a faraway look in his eyes. 'Not far now.'

28

Benny and I caught the bus up from Lismore to Nimbin and headed straight to Grandma's Farm, a small homestay on the fringes of town. After lugging our now more modest collection of possessions into a communal sleeping area, we caught up with a few locals I'd come to know over the preceding years and then got smashed on the local weed.

Nimbin marijuana is famous the world over for being a particularly smooth, strong bush weed. If you weren't a complete blow-in, the locals would look after you. There was no police station in Nimbin back then, the hotel still operated as a hotel rather than the backpackers' hostel it has become, and there were no tourist buses flooding the streets each day with fresh loads of young people from around the world, all doing the east coast of Australia. I'm not saying it was better or worse, just that it was different. It was quiet. Life was very slow. You might get twenty people in the Rainbow Cafe playing acoustic guitar and smoking some weed, but it just seemed like the thing everyone did rather than being something which drew a crowd of onlookers.

After a few days in town getting over the epic road trip that had delivered Benny and me to Nimbin, I hooked up with a very obliging girl who owned a Holden station wagon and we decided, on a stoner's whim, to head into Byron Bay for a night of debauched pleasure.

On a personal level, I wasn't travelling well. Since getting to Nimbin I'd been completely shit-faced on weed and booze and it wasn't long before any plans Benny and I might have had about getting our act together seemed as distant as ever. Plus, I was still hanging out from the smack, which by now had become such a regular physical sensation that I wasn't sure how I'd feel if I ever got completely free of opiates. Hanging out simply became a balancing act that I mediated each day to the best of my ability with whatever resources were at hand.

I don't remember much of what happened that night in Byron Bay. I know I got completely smashed and woke up in an unfamiliar room in an unfamiliar house in the main street at about five am. That was early for me, but I hated waking up somewhere completely strange so, after raiding the fridge, I set out for Nimbin.

Nimbin is about fifty kilometres from Byron Bay and I knew it wouldn't be easy getting one lift straight there, but I thought I'd be able to hitch-hike maybe three or four lifts and be home by breakfast. Five hours after setting out, however, walking all the while, I ended up just west of Bangalow and saw the signs for a drug rehab. I know some people might say, 'What are the chances of that happening?' And I can only say, not great. But that's what happened. And even more importantly, I walked into the joint and asked some questions.

What surprised me most about the person at the rehab clinic was how much they seemed to genuinely care about what I was going to do next. They asked me a whole series of questions and basically got my drug history down over the next hour. Then they laid out a plan for me: the first step required going to see someone for a referral to a detox unit, the second going to that detox for a week, after which I could hang out in rehab for anything up to six months.

It sounded like a good plan to me. Autumn was morphing into winter and I was riddled with lice from sleeping rough in Nimbin. I was also hungry most of the time because I couldn't get my shit together sufficiently to cook anything, and every time I did I just felt like more of a loser given what had happened to my glittering dreams of a career as a chef. A few months in rehab looked like a five-star option. Log fires were burning in the four separate rehab houses as well as the community hall, and because they only took up to twenty-four people at a time there seemed to be a lot of space for people to wander about and get themselves sorted. Obviously I still had absolutely no idea what a person did in rehab or detox, or what was required of someone once admitted, but it looked like a better deal than the one I had going on.

When I finally got back to Nimbin and told Benny what my plans were, he was a little put out. Though he agreed it would be the best thing for me to do, it meant his life was about to become considerably more difficult.

He would have to work out for himself what to do next and where to go. And I'm sorry to say things didn't go too well for Benny. Not long after I checked into Nimbin Hospital and spent a week detoxing, he made his way up to Queensland where, a year or so later, he crossed over that line between madness and whatever sanity is, and when he did he couldn't find his way back. He developed a crushing case of schizophrenia and things continued to deteriorate for him until eventually he found his way to a rehab which, like the one I went to, was a 'total abstinence' model. After they took him off his schizophrenia medication he went and jumped off a bridge.

For me, though, that time in Nimbin became a turning point as I finally got straight and managed to claw back something of a life. The total-abstinence model isn't for everyone, though. It didn't suit Benny, and in fact probably helped bring about his demise. There's no easy, one-size-fits-all cure for drug addiction or mental illness. Really, we know very little about the mind and its inner workings, though specialists in these fields have made huge advances in treating mental illness and addiction pharmacologically, and to turn away from those advances to pursue some abstinence, moral-fortitude model rarely works.

Interestingly, the word 'hospitality' derives from the same word as 'hospital'. The Latin *hospes*, or host, is also the root word for hotel and hostel. And what was interesting about that as I lay in a hospital bed in Nimbin was that it was difficult not to be aware of how similar hospitals and hotels are in the way they both deal with the human body. They both provide beds, food, drink and a sense of being looked after.

What illustrated this point most clearly for me was that on each of the seven nights I was in Nimbin Hospital someone would invariably wake us all up (there were only about twelve beds in the place) by banging on the locked front door of the old Queenslander and screaming out in pain. On my first night there, I thought something terrible must have happened—a car crash, a knife fight, or something like that. But the matron simply stomped to the locked door and yelled back at 'Eric' to piss off back to his snake pit and die there, and if he didn't go away she'd call 'John'. It was made clear to me over the following nights and days that hospitality is of enormous value to certain people at certain times in their lives. Indeed, while hospitality might be thought of as fulfilling the most basic of needs, true hospitality is a rare and precious commodity when a person has no obvious means of acquiring food, drink or shelter.

The first rule I learnt at rehab was that everyone had to let go of their various fronts and work identities in order to make contact with the real person inside them. And this applied to everyone. If you were a rock star, you were to refrain from playing the guitar or bursting into song. And if Mr or Mrs Rock Star couldn't resist the urge to sing in the shower, well then, that was a bust and they had to discuss how an inability to modify their behaviour in a safe environment like rehab might translate in the real world, where alcohol and drugs are available on every street corner. Each such bust was used as a starting point to build an awareness around patterns of behaviour. And that awareness was encouraged and discussed and built upon by both the individual and others in the community in order to lead people to an understanding about what their particular issues and triggers were in regards to being an addict. In this brave new world, drugs were simply a symptom of other, unresolved issues.

It wasn't just rock stars that needed to desist from banging the drum; bus drivers were not allowed to drive buses, surfers to surf, photographers to take pictures or hairdressers to cut hair. But they seemed to make an exception if you were a chef. In that case, you were encouraged to disappear into the community kitchen and do what you could with the stale adzuki beans and, on one particular day, Jerry. Jerry was the former rehab pet lamb that Stacey had become obsessed with. It seemed the idea of Jerry lying vacuum-packed at the bottom of the Tuckerbox freezer was something of an issue for Stacey, who was not really coping with Jerry's demise or life generally. And pretty soon the narrative of Stacey and her relationship to food became a topic that morphed into a theme that evolved into an issue that everyone talked about endlessly. Life in rehab was complex. Some days it took everything you had just to keep up.

The other thing I learnt pretty early on was that total abstinence meant no drugs or alcohol. Seems obvious, I know, but at the time I thought I might be able to convince the good folks at the rehab facility that my problem was no so much pot and alcohol as heroin. However, after confessing to smoking my last few spliffs up at the rehab's water tower, the community organised a meeting and decided to send me off for another week of detox.

I was to learn that this wasn't an uncommon phenomenon; junkies—or addicts, as everyone is known in rehab—are prone to not doing as they are advised and often find themselves doing multiple circuits of detox and rehab units, generally falling over just before the finish line. Not surprisingly, people who are given to taking lots of drugs and drinking too much alcohol seem to have a predisposition to failing at the total abstinence model of 'recovery'. When your whole identity has been wrapped up with the secret life of drug addiction, the idea of becoming a teetotaller isn't very appealing.

Obviously not everyone who goes to rehab is going to stay off the drugs when they get out. And often it's the painfully perfectionist recovering addict, the one who turns getting clean into a competition based on hours, days, weeks and months, that, come check-out time, finds themselves inexplicably heading back up to the Cross for a fresh look at Desperate Hour. And I can relate to that. But after cottoning on to what total abstinence actually entailed, and what would be required of me in order to spend a few months in rehab, I decided I would play the game for a while. Other than that, I promised myself nothing.

What playing the game meant was that I would make drugs and alcohol my number-one problem in life, even though I felt they were actually lower down the list of my so-called problems. While it may have seemed obvious to others that drugs were in fact my number-one problem, it wasn't that obvious to me at the time. I knew I had issues with smack, I drank like a fish and smoked like a V8, but when I was called upon to describe what an addict looked like, my image was always of someone older and more beat up than me. I pictured someone who'd done a lot of jail time and was covered in tatts—as opposed to the few pieces of amateur body art I had going on. An addict was always someone further along the path to complete and utter fucked-up-ness than me. I could point out other addicts—fuck me, look at that poor bastard over there, of course *he's* an addict. That woman who has turned up once too often on the streets at sunset, she's definitely an addict—and from the look of her a prostitute too. But me? I was just a young bloke down on his luck. All chefs used drugs, I'd reason. And I'd never used as much as him or her or them.

And yet, saying, 'Fuck it, I'll please these Johnnies in here and take this shit seriously for a while'—primarily because I had nowhere else to live—enabled me to get a few months' clean time during which I actually began to feel like a semi-normal human being again. I started to slow down a little; my thoughts ceased to be quite so mad and frenetic; the crazy voices in my head thinned out and a more realistic set of thoughts started to emerge. It wasn't super-pleasant at times but it wasn't as bad or as 'deep' as I thought it was going to be. Really, the rest of it, including whatever emotional catharses I might have had, whatever talking to counsellors I did about various things I might have done or were done to me, was small beer in relation to getting off the drugs.

I wouldn't have thought this was the case prior to going into rehab but the simple step of treating drugs and alcohol as my number-one problem, rather than any of the other shit, allowed any problems I might have had, or thought I had, to slowly sort themselves out. Life came back to me; it wasn't like I had to figure everything out, I just got caught up in the slipstream of things. And I can't really describe the sensation of living without any drugs floating around my system other than to suggest . . . it was like being a kid again, but different.

After the three months I spent working in the rehab community kitchen on no pay and little thanks, I was glad to be heading back to Sydney. There were three of us who got our tickets to leave on the same day and we all headed back to the city on the overnight bus. The rehab had a halfway house in Surry Hills where we could stay for a few months until we got our shit together and moved back into life proper. In many ways, the halfway house was the acid test. Most people don't handle the transition to city life at all well after being in rehab for several months. The sheer pace and energy of the city can overwhelm the good intentions of the vast majority of cleanskins.

I'm not sure if there's any formula about these things, it seems to just depend on the person and their capacity to adapt back to life without drugs. Some of our bunch died, some carved out fortunes and some just poked along either back on the gear or in a new job somewhere. A big problem after being clean for a few months—and some people had done nine months in rehab rather than my more modest three—was that people's tolerance for their particular drug of choice was right back down. But even more weird than that was, after a sustained break from using, it only took a very short time for tolerance levels to get back up to where they'd been previously.

The idea that a person can get clean and then slowly start using again, spending a few pleasurable months or years getting back to the point of madness, just doesn't happen. Based on personal experience and watching others, it takes about a week to get right back to wherever your last rabbit left you. And after a week of using again, it's as if you never left the scene. You might have a few new stories to share with your junkie mates about the freaks in rehab, but the gap between stopping using and starting using is like a weird dream: like it never happened at all.

29

There's a palpable tension in the kitchen at Rae's that no one wants to talk about.

Jesse's modus operandi over the last little while has been to piss everyone off with lax behaviour and then try to amend the situation. Each time he repents, the other chefs allow themselves to believe that he's finally left his bullshit ways behind and turned a corner on whatever the fuck is bothering him.

The main reason everyone is still sticking by him is because for the two years prior to this Jesse was a pretty reliable guy. The old Jesse might have gone too hard one night and had a blow-out, but he'd spring back and be careful to leave sufficient space between this and his next fall from grace. The new Jesse has been crashing and burning every other day, only to pull himself together at the last minute and save himself from complete humiliation.

But lately, instead of going for a five-minute cigarette break he's been going out for much longer, and this time he's been gone for over twenty minutes. It's infuriating for the other chefs in the kitchen and it's giving me the shits. Maybe it's because Carla is in the house and I know how much she wants a permanent job on the line, or maybe I'm just beyond caring about Jesse's problems any more, but I resolve that I'll let him go at the end of service. Having a few weeks or months off will allow him to resolve whatever is going on and provide him with the opportunity to start again somewhere new and different. The idea of a fresh start for Jesse is about as close as I can get to the idea of giving him another chance.

I got plenty of fresh starts when I was his age. And while it's always difficult being sacked or let go or laid off, it wasn't the end of me. In fact, sometimes it was the best thing that could have happened because it forced me to look at how my life was going. There were very few times I was happy with the picture that painted but, still, I got through and Jesse was going to have to find a way to get through as well.

I'll look after him by writing a decent reference. Good references count for a lot in hospitality because chefs, more often than not, don't stay in a job long enough to warrant the head chef writing them a reference. Chefs like Jesse tend to walk when the pressure, or the crew, or the girls—and the girls are the worst of it—get too much to bear. And walking after service on a particularly bad day may just involve a chef getting his knives together, collecting his bag from wherever it is, and disappearing. More often than not you see these chefs again, either down at the pub or in another kitchen somewhere. The hospitality industry is like that if you stick around long enough. And it's not hard for that sort of behaviour to become a habit, particularly if you've managed to collect a couple of decent written references along the way. The chefs who walk out of a joint after a few weeks or months, leaving everyone behind to pick up the pieces as a result of their hasty departure, never mention their previous walk-outs to the head chef in the new place. And even the most Teflon of kitchen cowboys can manage to get a decent pile of references together to at least create the impression they're a team player.

'Do you think I upset Jesse by talking about his father?' Carla asks, clearly worried.

'Even if you did, Carla, it doesn't excuse this bullshit. Can you start full time tomorrow?' I ask.

'On the line?' she asks.

'Yeah.'

'Sure.'

'It might even be tonight. Is everyone okay to clean the place up if Jesse doesn't come back in tonight?' I ask.

'Oh, fuck, Chef,' Soda says.

'I'm right,' responds Choc, who is completely over being shunted around different sections of the kitchen due to Jesse's recent lack of focus.

And even though I'm seriously thinking about leaving Rae's myself, I can't not deal with the Jesse situation. In fact, in many ways, I think my reticence to deal with Jesse's fucked-up behaviour is the reason I've convinced myself to slip out the door in a couple of weeks. And it's the wrong way to be thinking. Nothing good ever happened for me by pretending a situation was better than it was.

Soda looks at Choc for a beat, then glances at Carla and makes his decision.

'I don't know, Chef . . . I'll have to talk to Jesse,' says Soda, not pleased with the prospect of turning up to work without his mentor in the kitchen.

'Will you do the next week even if you decide to leave after that?' I ask.

Soda is the one I've been most worried about if I sack Jesse. I don't want to lose them both; I can't afford to lose them both at the same time and do another day, let alone two weeks.

'He's been out there for over twenty-five minutes now, Soda. The joke's over, mate,' I say.

Soda looks around the kitchen at everyone, his blue eyes unhappy. 'I'll do one week, for sure—but after that . . .' He shrugs.

'That's fine, Soda. I understand he's your friend. But I just can't run the kitchen with this bullshit any more,' I say, putting down my knife. 'Thanks for doing the week. I'm going out to talk to him.'

I take off my apron and walk out of the kitchen, stopping off in the restaurant to tell Scotty what I'm about to do. The restaurant looks a picture, all flickering candles in petite glass bowls, polished cutlery and pink frangipanis.

'Fuck him, Chef,' Scotty says, shaking his head. 'You've carried that prick for a couple of months now.'

'He hasn't been going bad that long,' I protest.

'Bullshit! He's been pleasing himself for at least a couple of months. It's no good for the rest of the team. They lose respect.'

'He's not a bad kid, Scotty,' I say, half hoping he might change my mind on what I'm about to do.

'Yeah, well, go have a beer with him tomorrow. This is work, mate. Vinnie would have cut him loose six months ago.'

I might have given Jesse more scope to mess up than Vinnie or Scotty or anyone else would have, but that's my right and privilege. Jesse was a team man from day one, backing me up every step of the way. So it's truly awful to be contemplating sacking him.

As I walk up the tunnel it's difficult not to reflect on all the other times I've had to do this. It's not something I enjoy but there are times when it's easier than others, and this is probably the hardest. The reason I've let thing slide so long with Jesse is because I was just like him when I was his age. Even if he thinks I have absolutely no idea what he's doing, I know what's around every corner he turns, over every rise. The thing is, you can't tell anyone anything when they're in the zone like Jesse is and I was. The words just float through you like so much hot air.

I check the toilets in the hope that he might be sick but he's not in there. He's not in the coolroom either, so I walk out towards the pool, but he's not in the Moroccan hut. Which is weird. I really can't see Jesse just running off home or into town after coming to work in such a positive frame of mind only an hour or so ago. I push open the back gate and step into the small patch of rainforest. It's already getting dark out here, beneath the canopy of trees, but I catch sight of Jesse sitting on the same log Choc was perched on earlier today.

'Fuck, Jesse! It's been half an hour!' I explode, suddenly furious.

Walking closer, I see that Jesse is slumped back into a branch. And as my eyes adjust to the light, I see he has a syringe dangling out of the crook of his left arm and a tourniquet wrapped around his left bicep.

'Jesse,' I shout, reaching out for him. 'Hey!' I rip the syringe out of his arm, loosen the tourniquet and go to lift him off the log. He falls heavily to the damp ground.

'Jesse!' I shriek, slapping him hard across the face.

Nothing: except Alice's weird text message flashing through my mind.

'Jesse!' I cry again, hoping my voice might carry back through the gate.

But it's like I'm in another world out here, a secret garden covered in skin; like a drum my voice will never break.

'Jesse,' I say, shaking him, like, *don't be a fuckwit.*

'Scotty!' I scream. 'Soda!' I'm aware of not wanting to upset the hotel guests, which is not something I should be worrying about. But I see what they'll see. I see the workers pulling focus onto themselves and distracting the guests from their good time. I see their faint disgust, their barely disguised annoyance. This is not what they paid a thousand dollars a night for.

'C'mon, Jesse, breathe!' I'm repeating what the doctor said to me in St Vincent's all those years ago. It had worked for me. I breathed in deep. I'd been searching for something . . . unaware of what it was . . . until the doctor's command gave me a focus, his voice breaking through my confusion to locate the source of my hunger.

His command insisting that I allow my lungs to take possession of their object of desire. It was like I needed to be reminded to do something I'd never had to think about doing before.

'Breathe!' I order Jesse.

But Jesse looks tired. And peaceful. Dreamy. Entranced.

'Scotty!' I yell again.

Upstairs, in the guest rooms that wrap around the pool, the silhouettes of the fortunate play out their roles across slight white curtains, oblivious to the drama below. The sound of the pool pump and air-conditioners and the hot-water systems and running taps seem to crowd out my voice. Sounds of insects and birds and cars muffle my cries.

I concentrate on giving Jesse mouth to mouth; I push the palm of my hand into his rib cage. I repeat everything, over and over and over. Like a machine. Like I know I must. I scream out. I continue CPR for minute after minute. I count out the repetitive actions in my head.

I'm beside the Memorial Baths in Rockhampton gaining a Bronze Medallion. I'm twelve years old again. I remember everything I was trained to do. Hand over hand, I press one thousand and one, one thousand and two, one thousand and three into Jesse's flat chest.

'Help!' I yell. I'm just a kid again. Helpless. 'Help!' I cry.

But no one arrives.

Jesse is cold. He's deep blue and icy cold. He's dead. The various processes of death have taken over his body. It's like all my training was for nothing. It's like . . . the end of something and the beginning of something else.

After a while I stop and look at Jesse in disbelief. How did this happen?

I am disgusted with myself that I left him out here so long; that I didn't listen to the loudest voice in my head as the minutes ticked over in the kitchen, the voice that insisted I come stomping out here, kicking and screaming and yelling.

You stupid, stupid kid, I'm thinking. I smooth his fringe across his face the way I know he likes it; to make it like the photo he has of himself inside his mind.

I resolve there is no emergency. I feel a powerful need to talk with Alice.

I push back through the gate into Rae's. I walk back through the tunnel to the phone in the kitchen. I am not sobbing, but tears run down my face. I call an ambulance. Then I call the cops, though Jesse would hate them seeing him like this. Then I call Alice and tell her what happened. She's devastated. She understands. She knew something had to give; she says to be careful driving home.

Scotty and the boys slowly gravitate towards me as I talk on the phone. They hear my conversation with the operator as I request an ambulance and tell them why I need it. Then Soda runs down the tunnel, clattering over the floorboards which Vinnie installed cheaply in order to give some semblance of designer decor between the restaurant and the male toilets. And it's strange that at this moment I feel resentment at Vinnie's choice of materials to refurbish the tunnel. It's not my name over the door.

I walk back out to the patch of rainforest. Scotty, Choc and Carla follow me. It feels more damp than it did a couple of minutes ago. Leaves rot in shadowy spaces. Ants are everywhere and they're already beginning to crawl over Jesse. I imagine a shrine. It's too early. I imagine Jesse's funeral: it's too early, impolite. I think of service tonight, of the customers, the rush, the adrenaline. And it's all too late.

Soda is doing CPR, just like I did. He's screaming at Jesse to wake up, to snap out of it. No one knew Jesse had been using heroin. How long had he been on the gear? How could he? Why didn't he talk about it? And the worst thing for me as a former user was how much sense it made of all his behaviour. Of course Jesse was on the smack. Everything fitted. This was the moment we'd all been waiting for. It wasn't me sacking him. It shouldn't have come to this but it's strange how you can feel a moment unravel. We thought he just needed more time, more love, some understanding. But all along he had a secret, a new love, a new best friend and a reason for living.

And now he's dead.

Scotty takes over from Soda with the CPR for a couple of minutes. He's serious, focused, but it's obvious his efforts are useless. Everyone knows it's just about doing something. And when he finally gives up and collapses onto the damp ground, Soda takes over again, insisting it isn't too late. No one wants to let go. We can't. We love him.

Everyone's distraught. The sirens sound. Choc walks out of the forest to guide the paramedics to where we all are. It's dark by now. Torches are shining, and people are speaking with gentle authority. The paramedics seem to feel the waste, the sadness and the absurdity of such a short life: the dreadful, pressing, knowing that it didn't have to be this way; the shame that it is.

As Jesse's body is loaded onto a stretcher, I feel strongly that I don't want to leave him alone. That it's my obligation to travel with him to wherever he has to go. I feel compelled to explain things to various people.

'I'm going with him,' I say, taking hold of the stretcher as if to add weight to my statement. After they slide Jesse's body onto a silver trolley, one of the ambulance officers ushers me into the back of the wagon.

It's strange watching them work on Jesse's body in the back of the ambulance. And what's most odd about it is how I seem to know everything they are doing. How does that happen? It's not as if I was ever conscious when I ended up in the back of an ambulance. Maybe it's from watching too much television? From always knowing when I used that I was only ever a heartbeat away from where Jesse is now: dead in the back of a meat wagon.

The sirens are on but there's no great rush, no panic. There'll be no miracle. The paramedics reckon Jesse's been dead for about twenty minutes. They show respect to me, out of respect for the dead. I feel deeply ashamed, enraged and grief-stricken. I'm crying, shaking my head.

'I can't believe he did this,' I tell the paramedics.

They shake their heads. They know. They've seen it all before.

'He's been in before, you know,' says the driver.

'What do you mean?' I ask.

'He's overdosed before. Jesse, isn't it?'

'Yeah,' I tell him. 'Jesse.'

'He's overdosed a couple of times,' the driver tells me. 'I didn't think we'd get him back last time but he responded to the narcane.'

'He was gone too long this time,' the guy in the back says. 'It's a time thing.'

'I couldn't . . . I didn't want to go out . . .' I say.

'Mate,' the guy in the back says, 'he's the one sticking needles in his arms. That's the risk junkies take.'

'He's not a junkie,' I say. They've got Jesse all wrong.

'Intravenous drug user,' the driver suggests politely. Like he doesn't want to upset me. Like he knows the truth is hard to bear.

'Jesus!' I say. 'I was a fucking junkie, mate. I used more than this little cunt spilt.'

'Did you give him the dope?' the driver asks.

'No!' I yell. 'I haven't used since I was a kid.'

'Did you know Jesse was using?' the guy in the back asks.

'No,' I say, shaking my head. For such an expert, I don't know much about anything. 'No,' I say again. 'I didn't know Jesse was using.'

In a flash I recall all the times I used smack. I recall all the different kitchens, all the lies, all the dirty, blunt syringes; the chemical smell of hospital wipes, of bleach. All the times I tried to redeem myself to all the different head chefs, governors and restaurant owners. I remember all the times I lied, because I had a secret.

The driver calls in to the hospital that he has a

DOA. He's respectful, upset even, as he speaks into the radio.

Dead on arrival. Jesse. But Jesse's just a kid, for fuck's sake.

'You can't . . .' I begin, but I can't continue. I'm over-whelmed. Like I haven't been for such a long time. I want to protect Jesse's legacy, how he'll be remembered.

Inside the hospital I'm asked to wait. I sit in the public lounge with mothers waiting to have their sick babies seen to, backpackers with blisters they need busted and dressed. There are no screaming emergencies, no chaos. Jesse is the lead story and I am his witness, yet even to me the staff are relaxed, calm; they don't want to upset me any more than I am. I know they'll perform whatever procedures they have to with Jesse, with his body. And I know it will all come to nothing.

It doesn't take long for the doctor to come out. Ten minutes, maybe twelve. The boxes are ticked and the circles crossed.

'Are you related?' the doctor asks.

'No, mate, I'm his boss,' I say.

'What's your name?' the doctor asks.

'Jimmy,' I tell him.

'Well, I'm sorry, Jim,' he says. 'He's gone. I have to phone his parents. Do you have their number?'

'No,' I say, slapping at my pockets, as if for some reason I might.

'That's all right. He's a local. We'll have his number here somewhere,' the doctor assures me. 'There's nothing more you can do now. I'm going to phone his parents and organise what needs to be done. You might have

to make a statement to the police—they should be here
soon.'

'Okay.'

And suddenly it's like, *I know, Doc, I've seen it all
before.*

30

The weeks that followed Jesse's death were like the early days of Alice and me all over again. Only this time she set the table, cooked and cleaned, settled the kids and listened. It felt in some ways that my life had come full circle. I started off by telling her every little thing to do with Jesse, about how this led to that and what everything meant . . . and then, when the words ran out, I just let go and floated down. I stared up at Alice and the boys, who seemed so large and alive; so full of energy and laughter and tears and petty resentments and love. And I knew they were worried that they couldn't reach me, that I was there but someplace else.

My mind raced back across time. I ran through all the ways in which I knew Jesse, all the times I could have said something but didn't—because what do you tell a kid who's determined to find out for himself? I remembered all the effort we put into crazy dishes and ridiculous menus; how he'd cough when he was anxious and pull at his hair when he was thinking. And I couldn't help but recall all the other times I'd spent in hospitality; what led me to Rae's and Alice and Jesse. What hospitality meant to me. How was it that I'd spent so many years cooking other people's dinner. It seemed such a bizarre thing to do.

When my mother organised the job for me at Oliver's all those years ago, I could not have guessed at the ramifications of her decision. And it wasn't that hospitality inspired me to become a great chef—that's someone else's story. The thing I realised most of all was that hospitality had always held a space for me. It was the home I never had: like all this time I was actually the guest, dressed in checks, working out the back. How many kitchens had I walked into and started work, heating, chopping, bending, inventing? How many times had I been shown something new? Watched a young kid's eyes light up when I taught the same thing to him or her years later? How many steaks had I cooked? Pans had I tossed? And why?

It seemed to me that people's ideas about what hospitality means are formed by their experiences of home. I felt strongly that Jesse's death and my youthful misadventures spoke to what it meant to be a child, a dependent being. I recalled all of my childish expectations, hopes and desires and recollections of pleasure. I felt ripped off that hospitality hadn't held a space for Jesse; at least, not like it did for me. Hospitality is primal; it speaks to nerves and pleasures and senses, rather than to languages, laws and numbers. And while for some people their desire is to transfigure hospitality into something scientific, when the sun goes down it is our bodies that require sustenance and sleep. Tables, chairs, beds, shelter, food, bathrooms . . . these are the base elements of what the human body requires for comfort. Not to address these things, or to address them in such a way that is somehow extraneous to hospitality, is to misunderstand what hospitality is.

It has never ceased to amaze me the impact that good food and a pleasurable dining experience can have on a person. So many people choose a restaurant as the place to seduce someone, to ask their lover to marry them, or blow up and fight with them. So many people have the time of their lives or settle large business deals over a great dinner out. Hospitality is a place where pleasure has not just a right to exist, but an obligation to be recognised.

I needed to find a reason to keep cooking after Jesse died; a reason to stand at the stove and suck up the pressure and push out the plates. A reason to train one more kid to cook a steak. And I'm not sure I found one convincing answer, but I did find a reason to smile again and trust fate's hand. When Alice and the boys finally did reach down and pull me up, I understood that it was our memories that mattered now. What we made of our lives with each other was all that really counted. It was the feelings that we shared that would form the stories of our lives.

In different ways, all of the crew felt responsible for Jesse dying. Vinnie shut the restaurant down for a few days out of respect and organised for someone to cook for the hotel guests. Like the rest of us, Vinnie needed some time to regroup. We all hung out for a while. We organised the funeral. We were as close as a crew could get. But there was no way we were ever going to be able to bring back the magic. We'd done nearly three years together and I'd done a year before that trying to get things to click. We'd created our version of what the best of hospitality looks and tastes and smells like.

Soda didn't say much after Jesse died. He just got more and more distant and, of all of us, he seemed to feel most responsible for what happened. He and Jesse had had an unspoken bond. He knew Jesse needed us more than he liked to let on. The younger chefs looked up to Jesse, he was the leader of their pack, and while he might have spent most of his time pushing them away, telling them they annoyed him, everyone knew he was nothing without them.

Soda didn't speak at the funeral or talk to anyone at the wake. He just hung around with a drink in his hand until he thought it was acceptable to leave.

Like a lot of chefs, Jesse didn't rate his family experiences all that highly. And maybe that's why certain kids are drawn into hospitality in the first place: to create a space that represents the home they wish they'd had.

The last thing Soda said to me before he got on a bus out of Byron Bay was that he was finished with cooking. He was going to try something else for a while. I never did see him again. I figure he found his way to a new place and found a niche somewhere, like people do. Every now and then I catch myself thinking about him, wondering how life turned out for him after Rae's.

It's not for everyone, the uniform of a chef. Restaurant kitchens are a world apart, cultural spaces with strict hierarchies and military traditions that are driven by passion, creativity and the eternal need that human beings have to eat and drink. Each day is a new challenge, starting again with fresh deliveries of produce, meats, seafood and dry goods. And it never ends: the restocking, cooking, menu planning, baking, sifting and boiling. It's like living in a constant state of becoming; like soon, everything is going to be organised. Only it never is.

Choc didn't stray far from home. He moved to another restaurant in the area. It was a good joint, with honest food, and no doubt he'll continue to learn and do well. The menu he's cooking now is Mediterranean rather than the modern Thai we were doing at Rae's. And Choc will be a better chef for having worked with another cuisine. Of all the kids, Choc was the one who was most stable. He had a mother who took an interest in everything he did. She was concerned for his wellbeing and was capable of predicting when he was about to lose the plot or crash and burn, and she took it upon herself to communicate with me about his limits and thresholds. The difference it makes for a kid to have a parent who is prepared to engage with the world on their behalf can sometimes be the difference between life and death. Not that any apprentice I've ever met wants their mum or dad embarrassing them by turning up to work unannounced, but it's a fragile time, those first few years out of school. The rules change and not everyone makes the transition as well or as easily as they thought they might.

The thing with Choc is that because he was such a good kid, he could slip under the radar at Rae's. He had the personality that never went searching for the spotlight and it paid to pull him aside every now and again and insist he answer a few questions about what the fuck was going on. Every time I did that to him he got anxious, worried that he might be in trouble. But he got used to it and I think he even came to appreciate having a chat about various things; about the latest menu item in his section or where he was heading in life, questions about how cooking school was going or if his piece-of-shit car was still running. It suited him to do a large chunk of his apprenticeship at Rae's, which as a kitchen managed to function around some personalities that rolled with very squeaky wheels. He was able to experiment with a lot of different things and when those things didn't turn out quite right, no one noticed until he'd fixed them up.

There wasn't a great handover between crews. Vinnie understood. He didn't expect me to go back at all after the funeral and I didn't really, at least not with any conviction. I sorted through some stuff, picked up my knives, gathered together my books and recipes, and faded away as the new crew started boiling stocks and sauces and complaining about the grease behind the stove.

Carla stayed on and became expert in all things Rae's—the link with the past. It was Carla who rang me after I'd left and drew various recipes out of me and asked about different cooking methods that involved pork belly or soft-shell crabs, silken tofu or oxtail. Her value to the new crew lay not only with her knowledge of all the local suppliers and where everything came from, but also with her ability to provide vital information about how Vinnie liked things.

It's weird how a crew falls apart, how after all the

effort to stave off chaos, everything just swirls about and changes anyway. And just like everywhere else I've ever worked, there was no stopping it at Rae's. But the upside to that realisation is the knowledge that hospitality is not so much some giant grinding industry as a time and a place created by a group of people. Restaurants come and go. None of the restaurants that I started out in twenty-five years ago are still around today. And in that light, it's not so much the industry of hospitality that has any real permanence, but more the life stories that sustain it. Chefs and wait staff and their creativity, their efforts and capacity to gel as a team, coupled with some architecture—a time and a place—describe what hospitality means. Hospitality is a people's palace, a space for our various bodies and their various needs. For the crew putting it all together, it's about hard work and impossible dreams, perfection, pleasure and the best of times.

Vinnie is still running things at Rae's. As a location it has lost none of its unique charm. I dropped in not long ago and the place was cruising along, like a palace beside the seaside might, like it has for the last fifteen years. Vinnie was the perfect host and it's a credit to him that he maintains the energy and enthusiasm to fuel his dream of what the best of hospitality looks like.

Sitting out in the restaurant again was cathartic. It was a perfect, blue, sunshiny day and the only thing missing was Scotty. Vinnie had sacked him—again. The news didn't surprise me and probably didn't surprise Scotty.

'You're not giving Scotty time off, are you, Vinnie?' I asked him.

'He's not coming back,' Vinnie said sternly.

'You were always too good to that bloke,' I said half jokingly, shaking my head.

'The food's a lot better too, since we got rid of you, Jimmy,' Vinnie said, in front of the new waiter he was training.

But he couldn't fool me. I could feel the love.

And the food that the new crew were doing was good. It wasn't as good as when we'd been kings. How could it be? We were the greatest. We created a time and place and our very own sense of how the best of times should look and feel and taste.

Vinnie and I didn't talk about Jesse. What could we say? That we loved him? That we still thought about him? That we wished he'd talked to us about what was going on? Of course we wished those things. But none of life's dramas are as important as we think they are when we're young, when everything's new for the first time. And you can't tell a kid who's keen to find things out for himself not to go where we've gone, not to touch the things we touched or feel the things we felt. No one could have stopped me doing anything until I was ready to stop. It's just that I was lucky and Jesse wasn't.

I'm still standing by a six-burner stove. I've moved a couple of times to mix things up. Alice won't let me get too stuck in one place any more. She's happy enough hooked up with a Teflon cowboy. And you never know . . . next time you're out to dinner and things are going okay, it just might be me or one of the guys pushing out the plates.

Acknowledgements

Sometimes in life there is nothing as important as finding someone who believes in you. My sincere thanks to Sean Barry, Mark Cherry, Tony Lewis and, especially, Alice, Kit and Sonny for believing in all my crazy dreams.

Many thanks to the Transforming Cultures Research Centre at UTS, in particular, Anne Cranny-Francis, Meredith Jones and Katrina Schlunke, who keep insisting I do nothing but my best work, and for lighting up unseen pathways.

I also need to thank Baden Offord at Southern Cross University for his generosity of spirit, inspirational teaching, and Zen leadership. Many thanks also to Janie Conway-Herron, who, as head of the writing program at SCU, was instrumental in me starting this story.

My sincere thanks to all the chefs I've worked with and met along the way. In particular, Heston Blumenthal, Jerome Clarke, Kylie Day, Cameron Gibb, Marty Gibb, Andrew Gimber, Zac Latinovic, Andy Wheeler, and 'Jesse', 'Choc' and 'Soda'. I do also need to thank one waiter, which is not easy for me . . . but life is short, so, thank you Scotty Wilson.

I especially need to thank Vinne Rae, who, as owner and executive chef of Rae's on Watego's, was generous enough to let me tell it how I saw it.

For their hospitality, goodwill and practical support, many thanks to Antony Alekna, David Bromley, Wendy Broome, Luke Burless, Greg Commerford, Barry Evans, Sue Hines, Marie Hook, Fiona Inglis, Rebecca Kaiser, Ali Lavau, Pippa Masson, Julianne Schultz, Erica Sontheimer, and especially Louise Thurtell, without whom, there would be no book.

I also need to thank my parents, for many things, but especially for having the grace and goodwill to let me tell things my way.